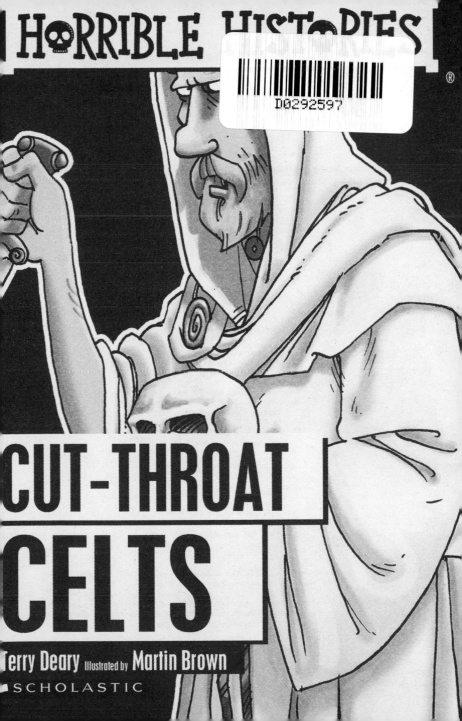

HORRIBLE HISTORIES

D0292597

CUT-THROAT CELTS

Terry Deary Illustrated by Martin Brown

SCHOLASTIC

With all good wishes and sincere thanks to Tracey Turner.

Scholastic Children's Books,
Euston House, 24 Eversholt Street,
London NW1 1DB, UK

A division of Scholastic Ltd
London ~ New York ~ Toronto ~ Sydney ~ Auckland
Mexico City ~ New Delhi ~ Hong Kong

First published in the UK by Scholastic Ltd, 1997
This edition published by Scholastic Ltd, 2016

Text © Terry Deary, 1997
Illustration © Martin Brown, 1997, 2016

All rights reserved. Moral rights asserted.

ISBN 978 1407 16540 0

Printed and bound by CPI Group (UK) Ltd, Croydon, CR0 4YY

10 9

www.scholastic.co.uk

CONTENTS

Introduction

History is horrible. Especially in school. Have you noticed how teachers never *tell* you anything? They *ask* you something and expect you to *know*!

They use funny new words and ask you to guess what they mean! How on earth can they expect that?

And they use posh words to describe the really horrible bits of history…

Then, just when there's a chance that history lessons may be getting interesting, the teacher stops and refuses to tell you the gory details.

Were the Celts really cut-throats? And why? And what did they do with those heads? What you need is a book that tells you the truth, the whole truth and nothing but the truth. What you need is a Horrible History of the cut-throat Celts!

Well! You lucky person! You just happen to have found one…

Timeline

750 BC The Ancient Greeks meet traders from Hallstatt (Austria). The Greeks say they call themselves Keltoi – dodgy spelling, but better than the Celts who can't write at all!

387 BC Now the Celts meet the Romans and beat them in battle. The Romans – also dodgy spellers – call them Celtae.

279 BC The Greeks drive the Celts out of Greece after the Battle of Delphi. The Greeks have the help of bad weather and landslides (which is cheating a bit).

225 BC At the Battle of Telemon in Greece the Romans beat the Celts.

218 BC The Carthaginians of North Africa attack the Romans in Italy and the Celts help them but...

202 BC The Romans beat the Carthaginians in Carthage and turn their attention to Celt lands in Spain and Northern Italy. Sweet Roman revenge.

60 BC Roman Julius Caesar decides to make a name for himself by taking over Celtic Gaul (France). Some Celts welcome him – others don't ... and are wiped out.

52 BC Vercingetorix leads a Celtic rebellion against Caesar. Romans win and rule France. Then they start looking across the English Channel…

AD 43 Emperor Claudius defeats the Celts in Britain. They're driven back to the hills of Wales and Scotland despite…

AD 61 A very bloody rebellion led by Queen Boudicca ends in another win for the Romans.

AD 84 Battle of Mons Graupius in Scotland and the last of the free Celts are now in Scotland and Ireland. The Romans rule, OK?

AD 120 Emperor Hadrian builds a wall across the North of England to keep the Pict and Scot Celts out … or to keep them in, depending on which way you look at it!

AD 312 Emperor Constantine becomes a Christian and the Roman Empire converts to Christianity. Even the Celts are converted and their old ways die. No more sacrifices.

AD 410 The Romans leave Britain but Angles, Saxons and Jutes rush in and settle before the free Celts can get back. A bit like musical chairs!

AD 432 St Patrick goes to Ireland and converts Irish Celts to Christianity.

AD 493 The British Celts make one last effort to drive out the Saxons and win the Battle of Badon. Their leader is the Awesome King Arthur … maybe.

AD 520 Awesome Arthur loses his last battle when he fights his own nephew … maybe. But while the British Celts are squabbling the Angles and Saxons take over the south-east of Britain and create Angle-land, or England. You may have heard of it.

Getting to know the cut-throat Celts

Nobody really knows where they came from. It was far too long ago. Some historians say there were Celts in Britain about 1180 BC – others say it was earlier. They came from central Europe and spread in all directions till they came up against the Romans.

Now the Romans were a single nation – the Celts were dozens of tribes who fought against each other as often as they joined together to fight the Romans. In the end some of these tribes were wiped out, some agreed to be ruled by the Romans and some were driven to the far corners of the known world – Ireland, Scotland, Wales, Cornwall, Brittany and the small Isle of Man. These communities of Celts survive to this day.

The thing that made them Celts was that they shared a language and they shared their legends and their customs. The Romans might have ruled them ... but the Romans were still pretty scared of them!

The Celts are terrifying in appearance with deep-sounding and very harsh voices. They use few words and speak in riddles. They often exaggerate with the aim of making themselves look good and making others look weak. They are boasters and threateners, yet they have quick minds and a natural ability for learning.

SAY I'M THE BEST OR I'LL BITE YOUR KNEECAPS OFF

Diodorus Siculus, 1st century BC

The largest Celt tribe that the Romans came up against were called Gauls…

> *Almost all of the Gauls are tall, fair and red-faced, terrible for the fierceness of their eyes, fond of quarrelling and of dreadful pride.*

Ammianus Marcellinus,
4th century AD

The Romans said some pretty spiteful things about the Celts, including…

> *When the Celts become drunk they fall into a deep sleep … or they fall into a terrible rage.*

Diodorus Siculus, 1st century BC

The ancient Celts were violent and loved arguing, but is it fair to call them 'cut-throat'? Maybe. Look at the evidence and decide for yourself.

THE CELTS HAVE A DISGUSTING AND ILLEGAL HABIT OF CUTTING OFF HEADS. IS THAT NOT TRUE?

THE WHOLE POWER OF A PERSON IS IN THE HEAD. EVEN A DEAD ENEMY CAN HARM YOU UNLESS YOU CUT OFF HIS HEAD, IT'S SELF DEFENCE

IS THAT THE ONLY REASON?

THERE IS ANOTHER ADVANTAGE IN CUTTING OFF AN ENEMY'S HEAD—WE BELIEVE YOU GAIN ALL THAT ENEMY'S WISDOM AND STRENGTH

IF THAT'S TRUE THEN HAVING CHICKEN FOR SUNDAY DINNER SHOULD MAKE YOU AS WISE AS A CHICKEN!

LOTS OF PEOPLE ARE!

THERE ARE STORIES ABOUT CELT WARRIORS INVADING A COUNTRY AND MARRYING ITS WOMEN. THEY SAY THE CELTS CUT OUT THE TONGUES OF THEIR NEW WIVES SO THE PURE LANGUAGE OF THE MEN WILL NOT BE SPOILED BY THE FOREIGN LANGUAGE OF THEIR NEW WIVES

THESE STORIES ARE FOUND ONLY IN LEGENDS BUT I CAN'T HELP WONDERING IF THE STORY-TELLERS HAD SOME TRUTH TO BASE THEIR GRUESOME TALES ON...

PROVE IT

A lot of people in Britain today have Celt blood flowing through their veins. If you are one of them then be glad your blood is staying in your veins and not decorating the wall of some hill-fort hall. Be glad you'll never meet an ancient Celt!

Lousy legends

Poets were highly respected in the Celt world – like pop singers today. And, like pop singers, they were well paid. The bad news is that it was a long hard job to train as a Celtic poet. A pop singer probably trains for 12 whole minutes – a Celtic poet trained for 12 years.

Poets learned grammar and very long poems – 80 in the first six years. They learned another 95 in the next three years, and by the end of the 12 years' training they would know 350 story-poems ... if they survived, that is.

Because learning a story-poem an hour or so long took a lot of concentration. Have you ever had a teacher complain that you lack concentration? Did they nag you into concentrating? Think yourself lucky – you could have had a Celtic poetry teacher.

14

The poet travelled round with a metal model of a tree branch. It had bells on and they rang as he rode along or entered a feasting hall.

The branch told you what sort of poet he was – a bronze branch for a qualified poet, a silver branch for an expert and a gold branch for someone who was top of the pops.

He'd swagger around in a cloak covered in birds' feathers – the feathers of white and coloured birds were worn below the belt, the crests and necks of mallard ducks above the belt. Some say a swan's head dangled down his back (don't try making one of these – you'll just look quackers).

The poet expected to be well paid for his entertainment. If he wasn't then he was likely to compose a very sarcastic verse about the lord in charge. You know the sort of thing...

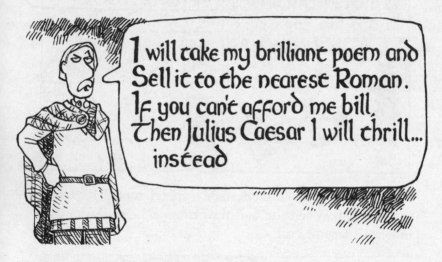

I will take my brilliant poem and Sell it to the nearest Roman. If you can't afford me bill, Then Julius Caesar I will thrill... instead

Never upset a king...
Of course some poets became too greedy and in AD 574 King Aed Mac Ainmirech banned all poets from Ireland. The King had a symbol of his power – a brooch in the shape of a wheel. Some poets got a bit cheeky and asked him for it. Lords often gave pieces of jewellery for a good story but the poets should never have asked for the wheel brooch – it

seemed like they were taking power away from the lords and the King. Saint Columba put in a good word for the poets and they were allowed to stay, but they never again asked for impossibly grand payments.

...and *never* upset a poet!

But be warned. It didn't pay to upset a poet. If he cursed you, you might...

- lose in battle
- break out in blisters
- speak only baby-talk.

MUMMY, MUMMY, THAT NASTY ARMY BEATED ME ALL UP, THEN I GOT BWISTERS ALL OVER

SOB

Terrible tales

Imagine the nastiest thing possible. That's the sort of thing the Celtic poets sang about. There's nothing wrong with the following story ... unless you're a member of the Pony Club and don't enjoy horse-burgers and chips.

Horses meant speed and beauty – they were linked to the Celtic Sun god. Celts believed that you could gain some of a horse's powers by eating it. (I've tried this. Does it work? Neigh!)

WARNING: Horse lovers should skip the following poem! It is loosely based on a Celtic poem ... very loosely. Well, to be honest, if it got any looser it would drop off.

17

The king was in his feasting house
Waiting to be crowned.
They killed a white horse, cut it up,
And stirred it round and round
Inside a cauldron great and deep
All filled with water, hot.
They ate the horse meat, not the bones,
Until they'd scoffed the lot.

(Well, when I say 'the lot', I mean
They didn't eat the saddle.)
The king stood up, and then he cried,
'My friends! It's time we paddled!'
The king's friends all took off their clothes
And jumped into the pot!
They splashed about in bones and soup,
And see how clean they got!

And when they all had washed and scrubbed,
They jumped back out again.
They drank the horse soup, every drop
Until the pot was drained.

Not much wrong with eating horse meat – the French do it all the time. But would you drink bath-water after all your smelly friends have bathed in it? Yeuch!

Batty beliefs

The Celts had gods all over the place – gods in trees, gods in streams and even gods in stones. The oak tree was especially holy and the mistletoe that grew on it was magical stuff. People today still believe this and that's why we have the Christmas custom of kissing under the mistletoe.

WARNING: Do not be tricked into kissing some snotty creep who happens to fancy you. Tell them the truth…

MISTLETOE IS ONLY MAGICAL WHEN IT IS CUT BY A DRUID USING A GOLD SICKLE

THAT MAKES *ME* SICKLE

Ten things you need to know about Druids

1 Laws were made by the kings, but it was the Druids who advised the king. This is rather like Government Ministers advising the Queen today. They are *her* laws – but everybody knows the Government runs the country. The Druids also acted as judges to enforce those laws. It didn't pay to upset a Druid.

2 Druids were clever clogs because they spent 20 years training to become one. This is even worse than modern schools where you spend 11 to 15 years training to be an adult. You then spend another 50 years wondering if it was worth it.

3 The sacred mistletoe must not touch the ground. When the Druid with the golden sickle climbed a tree, another two Druids stood below and caught it in a white cloth as he threw it down. (This was also very handy if the Druid with the golden sickle fell out of the tree!)

AND STANDING UNDER THE RIGHT TREE WOULD HELP TOO

4 These Druids were the village wise men (and maybe wise women) who advised the villagers on problems like the best time to plant their crops. They were like your local vicar but with an important difference. Your vicar might expect a five-pound note from each of his worshippers – a Druid expected blood. And the Druids had real power over the people. As Roman Julius Caesar said...

When a person disobeys a Druid then they ban them from attending at sacrifices. This is the cruellest punishment a Celt can suffer.

5 The Roman writer, Lucan, said Druids even sacrificed humans. Lucan claimed that, 'the trees were sprinkled with human blood.' Yeuch. Of course Lucan could have been exaggerating a bit ... or a lot. The Romans didn't like the Celts and may have written a few lies about them. Of course the Celts didn't do much writing, so the Roman stories have gone down in history and the truth has been forgotten.

6 The Celts of Gaul sent their Druids over to Britain to be trained. British Celt Druids must have been the best.

7 When a Druid wanted some spirit help he slaughtered a bull and had it skinned. Then he lay down on a bed of rowan branches and wrapped the bull's hide round him, bloody side next to him. As he slept he experienced dreams that answered his questions or solved his people's problems – problems like, 'How do you get blood stains out of a Druid's best robe?'

OF WHAT DID YOU DREAM O GREAT DRUID?

FOR SOME REASON, ALL THAT CAME INTO MY HEAD WAS LOADS OF FRESH HAY AND CHARGING AT RED THINGS

8 Druids were also fortune-tellers who said they could see into the future. What would you do if you could see into the future? Become a fortune-teller and make your fortune? Or simply pick next Saturday's winning lottery numbers – every week for a year? It's easy. All you have to do is follow the dreadful Druid method of divining the future.

• Take the flesh of a dog.

• Chew it.
• Call upon the spirit of the dog to give you its secret.
• Have a long deep sleep OR place the palms of your hands over your eyes, crossing your hands over your face.
• A vision will reveal the wisdom that is guarded by the animal.

The Celtic Druids used this method to predict who the next king would be. But why would a wise dog know that? You may not be able to get the flesh of a dog – maybe next door's Rottweiler doesn't want you to bite its leg – but the Celts believed the flesh of a cat or a bull would give up that animal's secret. Could a cat's flesh reveal winning scratch cards? (Cat's – scratch ... geddit? Oh, never mind.) Probably the flesh of a bull is easiest to get hold of. Chew that and soon you will either have the gift of prophecy or mad cow disease.

9 When the Christians arrived in the Celt world in the 5th century the Druids had to go. The Christians had spent a couple of hundred years being thrown to the lions and that put them off bloody sacrifices for life. You'd be surprised to learn that animal sacrifices were still being made in AD 868, wouldn't you? Then you will be astounded and gobsmacked to discover that they were still being made in AD 1868. That's right, just 130 years ago there was still a Celtic-style festival held in Cevennes in France. It involved throwing valuables and animals into a lake as offerings to the gods.

10 The Druids had some useful powers that you probably wish *you* had. They could...

• Change their shape to anything they wanted.

• Control the weather.

• Bring down mists to make themselves invisible.

• Travel through time.

Imagine that! There could be a Druid at your school. If your history teacher seems to know an awful lot about the Celts then maybe they *are* a Celt! A Druid on holiday in the 20th century. This is just one example of...

Horrible Historians

There's a dead man in the British Museum in London. Well, he's more a half-dead man because only half of his body is on show!

In 1984 a mechanical digger was cutting through turf in Lindow, Cheshire, when it came across this shrivelled body. Archaeologists and historians were excited by the discovery ... they have a very sick idea of excitement, you understand. They examined the body and said it was definitely a Celt. The chemicals in the swampy land had preserved him like a pickled onion in vinegar. The one and only Celtic face to be seen in modern times!

The historians then set about discovering who he was and how he died ... and it looked like a gruesome story. The man had well-shaped fingernails so he wasn't a peasant. And his death seems to have been some sort of cruel and cut-throat Celtic sacrifice. Maybe those rotten Romans were right about the Celts after all? Or maybe the victim deserved to die. We'll never know that.

What would you do with the Lindow man who was killed and dumped in a bog? Give him a nice burial and let him rest in peace? Put a headstone over his grave with a poem? Probably.

What have the horrible historians done with him? Stuck him in a glass case for people like you and me to gawp at. The least they could do was give him an epitaph – a message from the dead to the living. Maybe you could write one. This is just a suggestion...

The Lindow Lament, or The Man With No Name Who Wishes He Had One

*The Celts they came and took me in the middle of the
    night,*
And I knew if they meant business, I was dead.
*They never asked permission, said no 'Please,' or 'By
your*
    leave.'
They simply went and bashed me on the head.
(Twice)

They used a choking cord until they cut off all me breath,
They used me like some sacrificial goat.
When they were really sure that I was in the arms of
    death,
The rotten bleeders went and cut me throat.
(Messy)

So all you living people, see the fate that I was dealt.
Captured by the cruel and wicked Druids.
Think yourself dead lucky you don't have to face those
    Celts,
Who would drain you dry of all your body fluids.
(Blood)

They laid me here all shrivelled up — no peace, no grave,
    no name;
A wrinkled mummy cut off at the pelvis.
A label calls me 'Lindow Man', and that's my lasting
    fame.
I'd rather be a Percy, Joe ... or Elvis.
(Wouldn't you?)

Dreadful deaths

People of the Ancient world believed that all life was made up of four 'elements' – air, earth, fire and water. The Greeks were the first to put this idea down in writing around 2,500 years ago, and thinkers and doctors believed it till about 300 years ago.

The Celts believed it too. But the Ancient cut-throat Celts didn't stop at believing life could be explained by the four elements – they believed that death could too!

If there was a god of air then the Celts had to keep him or her happy by sacrificing someone using 'death by air' – suffocating, strangling or hanging. If there was a god of water then the sacrifice would be 'death by water' – drowning – and so on.

Which would you choose?

Obviously the Lindow man is proof that death by air was a Celtic form of execution or sacrifice.

The Roman leader Julius Caesar wrote about the Celts building huge basket-work models of men, filling them full of victims then setting fire to them. For hundreds of years historians have said that Caesar was lying. But many Celt legends include stories of victims being chained inside in an iron house which is then heated till it's red hot.

The Gaul goddess, Teutatis, was kept happy by having victims drowned in an iron cauldron, but that is only in legend. There's no proof that the Celts in Gaul actually did it. But there have been bodies found in swamps which have been covered with wooden panels. It is possible that the panels were used to hold the victim under the swamp until they drowned. No one is sure if the victims were sacrifices or criminals being executed.

No one has found a grave where a human appears to have been buried alive, but there was a nasty custom of bricking up an animal in the walls of a house to bring luck. Cats were often sacrificed in this way and in 1995 a mummified moggy was found in an old Northumberland house when it was being rebuilt. The cruel Celt custom was still being practised a hundred years ago!

Saints alive

In time the Celts dropped their gods of streams and woods and stones and became Christian. But a lot of their beliefs were carried forward into the new religion. They still had godlike humans who performed the most incredible miracles. People like Winifride and her Uncle Beuno.

Saint Gwenfrewi (or Winifride in English)

Winifride was the niece of Saint Beuno, an abbot in 6th-century Wales. Young Prince Caradoc ap Alyn loved her but she made it clear she did not want to marry him. This upset the young Prince from Wales so he drew his sword and cut off her head, as princes sometimes do when you upset them. As her head hit the ground there wasn't so much a splatt! as a splash! Because a spring of water gushed out of the dry rock.

Along came Saint Beuno, stuck her head back on her body and she was restored to life, with just a thin white line round her neck to show where she'd had her little accident. Beuno was not so kind to Caradoc. The saint cursed the Prince till the earth opened up and swallowed him. This taught him a lesson he'd never remember because he was dead before he could forget. Even his descendants suffered from Beuno's curse. They all barked like dogs until they made a pilgrimage to the well.

31

Winifride's well waters are now said to cure illnesses and the well is still visited by tourists. So, don't go upsetting a prince of Wales … unless your uncle is a saint.

Hope springs eternal

At one time heads must have been bouncing round Celtic lands like lottery numbers in a drum. Saint Llud, Saint Justinian, Saint Nectan and Saint Decuman all lost their heads and springs sprang as they fell. Saint Cadfan's shrine was set up in AD 516 and is said to cure rheumatism while Saint Canna's well water will soothe your stomach when you feel a gut ache coming on.

Saint Brigit was popular in all of the Celtic countries: Scotland, Wales, Cornwall, the Isle of Man and Brittany as well as her home in Ireland. She has so many wells it seems someone must have cut her head off and played football with it.

Brigit's crosses are still set up on farmland in Ireland to protect crops and animals. This is because she used to punish people who stole her cattle by drowning or scalding them. She didn't have Winifride's problem of princes chasing her because she made herself ugly by putting out one of her eyes.

Horrible historical joke:

WHY WAS SAINT BRIGIT LIKE A LONELY TEACHER?

BECAUSE SHE ONLY HAD ONE PUPIL

Saints un-alive

The Celts became such great Christians that they practically invented many of the great Christian traditions. It's said that John Cassian was a Celt born in Scythia and he brought the first monasteries to Europe. (He pinched the idea from the Egyptians, though.) The main thing needed to be a saint is to have...

- a very good life
- a very messy death
- an incredible miracle happen.

Some Celt saints managed all three!

Saint Teilo

Saint Teilo, a 6th-century Welsh saint, is buried at a place called Llandeilo Fawr ... and in Penally ... and in Llandaff Cathedral. This is not very difficult if you are a saint. And, no, they didn't chop him into three and share the bits out. In one night his corpse became three bodies. Don't you wish you could do this? You could send one body to school, while one went to the seaside and the other stayed in bed and watched television.

Saint Olcan

That's Ol-can ... *not* Oil-can. Olcan's father died before he was born – the shock killed his mother who also died before he was born. She was buried and THEN Olcan was born. A passing nobleman heard baby Olcan crying, dug him up and saved his life. Don't try this in your local cemetery – body-snatching is a grave offence.

Saint Ronan

Cornish monk Saint Ronan had a pretty rough life after he was dead. His body was loaded onto a wagon and the oxen pulling it were set free. Where the wagon stopped, Ronan would be buried. But as the cart trundled along it was attacked by an angry Celt woman – people say Ronan had upset her because he took no notice when she tried to chat him up! Anyway, first she

hit one of the oxen and knocked its horn off, then she hit Ronan's corpse a mighty smack in the face. He was probably glad to get safely under the ground after that!

Saint Monessa

This beautiful Irish Princess was a non-Christian Celt, but then she heard Saint Patrick preaching. She thought old Pat was wonderful and said, 'Convert me to Christianity! I want to be baptized if it's the last thing I do!' Patrick baptized her ... and it was the last thing she did. She died from the happiness. (Please note: If you die from happiness while reading this book your money will not be refunded.)

Saint Cieran

If you're a saint it is always handy if you can work miracles after you've died. Cieran managed it. It seems that all the other saints in Ireland were praying that he'd die young. Cieran didn't let them down. He was only 33 when he died of plague in AD 548 – there were plagues even before the famous 1349 Black Death and this one got him.

Dying was a very popular thing for Cieran to do and Saint Columba cheered. But Columba took a chunk of turf from Cieran's grave and carried it with him everywhere. Years later Columba was caught in a deadly whirlpool, threw the turf in the water and the whirlpool went calm.

Saint Mylor

Little Mylor was only seven when his dad was murdered. The bishops persuaded the killer not to murder Mylor too. He didn't. Instead he chopped off the boy's hand and foot. Mylor hopped along to the blacksmith and had a metal hand and foot made. Miraculously his flesh-and-blood hand grew back! But Mylor's guardian cut off his head next. The boy didn't

have a head-growing trick – or maybe the blacksmith didn't do heads – and he died. The murderer picked up the head happily – and dropped dead three days later.

Six dead funny facts
1 The Celts didn't mind dying too much. After all, they believed that when you left this life you woke up in the 'Otherworld'. The trouble is you could also die in the Otherworld ... then you were reborn into this world. Then you die and go to the Otherworld, then you're reborn, then you die ... (Once you've done this you will know how a yo-yo feels.)

2 The Celtic 'day' began at nightfall and ended with the fading light. Similarly the year began in November with the dying plants and sprang to life in the spring. It made sense to them to see Death as the start of your existence and Life as its end. (Well, it made sense to them, if not to you.)
3 This belief meant Celts would laugh at a funeral and cry at a birth. Christian Celts, even today, hold parties for the dead – called 'wakes' – and enjoy a good laugh at a funeral.

4 The Celts buried the dead person with some of their favourite belongings from *this* life – jewellery, weapons, clothes and, of course, food. Joints of pork seem to be the corpses' favourite food though sometimes calf, sheep and cattle bones have been found. (Personally I'd take a bag of crisps. What about you?)

5 They buried the very rich with a chariot. But the crafty Celts didn't waste a good chariot on a crumbling corpse. They usually buried a clapped-out chariot. Of course, the chariot needed a horse to pull it ... so the cut-throat Celts buried a clapped out horse along with it! (Archaeologists can tell the state of the horse by the condition of its teeth and bones.)

6 One wealthy Celt was buried with 40 litres of Italian wine! Just as well the Celts didn't have breath tests or he'd be banned from driving the chariot before he even got to the afterlife!

Weird war

The Celts were fierce fighters. Some of the stories about Celt warriors are reported by the Roman historians, so they are usually believed (why *is* it that people always believe horrible historians?). In fact the Romans probably exaggerated a bit to make their own soldiers look better when they defeated the Celts.

1 Cu Chulainn became temporarily insane in battle, going into warp-spasm when he was so full of blood-lust that he couldn't tell friend from foe. This strange frenzy can still be observed on soccer pitches today!

2 The early Celt warriors fought with no clothes on except perhaps a gold band around the neck called a torque. They didn't believe in wearing armour. The Celts knew their gods would decide if they were to die that day. All the armour in the world wouldn't protect them. The Romans were protected by armour ... and underpants!

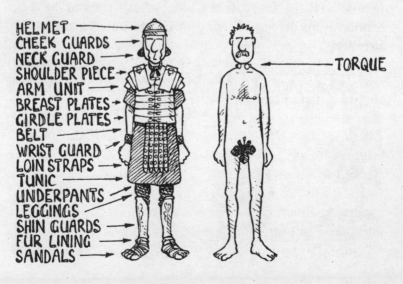

HELMET
CHEEK GUARDS
NECK GUARD
SHOULDER PIECE
ARM UNIT
BREAST PLATES
GIRDLE PLATES
BELT
WRIST GUARD
LOIN STRAPS
TUNIC
UNDERPANTS
LEGGINGS
SHIN GUARDS
FUR LINING
SANDALS

TORQUE

3 The Celts were very bad losers. If they looked like losing they killed themselves. This kind act saved their enemies the trouble. In one cheerful Roman statue a Celtic warrior is shown plunging a sword into his chest with one hand while holding his dead wife in the other. He has already killed her to save her from capture! Hope she was grateful!

4 The crafty Celts were great riders and invented a special saddle for fighting. They had no stirrups for their feet so there had always been a danger of the riders falling off. The Celt saddle of the 2nd and 3rd centuries BC had four high bumps (pommels is the posh word) that could be gripped with the legs. That left one hand free to guide the horse and the other to hold a weapon.

5 In AD 52 an army of 50,000 Romans defeated 250,000 Celt Gauls led by Vercingetorix. The trouble was the Celts ran wild in battle and fought as individuals. The Romans worked as a team and won.

6 The Celts liked fighting so much they didn't just fight against enemies … they fought against each other! They also had a bit of fun fighting for other people as far away as Egypt, Greece and Asia Minor.

7 The Romans were particularly shocked by rebel British leader, Boudicca. When her husband died he left his land to Emperor Nero and his daughters. The Emperor wanted it all and had Boudicca and the daughters flogged. Big Bad Boud attacked Roman towns and was especially cruel to women prisoners. They were executed and bits of their bodies were cut off and stuck in their mouths. They then had a sharp wooden stake pushed through their bodies and they were hoisted up for everyone to see. This nasty hobby became really popular 1,400 years later when a certain Count Dracula of Romania used it against his enemies…

8 And talking about Romania … a Celt chieftain's helmet found in Ciumesti (Romania) has a large model bird perched on top. Its wings are spread and are hinged in the middle so they can flap up and down! Historians believe the chieftain would only wear it on important occasions – not in battle. It's a bit like Long John Silver having a parrot on his shoulder, only not so messy!

9 There is no doubt that the Ancient Celts believed that the greatest prize in battle was an enemy's head. They decorated both their saddles and the doors of their houses with heads. They preserved old heads in cedar oil and brought them out every now and again to boast about them. Some boasted that they refused to part with their enemy heads even though they'd been offered the head's weight in gold.

10 The Celts believed that single combat was a good way to show off your bravery and settle an argument. Two heroes would step forward and begin by insulting each other!

Then they'd start fighting while the soldiers on both sides watched to see that they fought fairly.

Awesome Arthur

The Celts usually chose the best warrior as the leader of their tribe. If two warriors both claimed to be the best then they had to fight for the honour. One didn't have to kill the other one, just beat him in single combat.

The Celts didn't usually have fine crowns for their kings. But the winner of the battle needed some sign that he was the boss. This sign would often be a fine sword.

Before the fight, the great royal sword was placed on an altar stone. The Druid presented this sword to the winner. Anyone who tried to take the new king's power from him would be cursed by the magical power of the sword.

But here's the clever bit! Some historians believe this was how a Celt called Arthur took control of the kingdom! Everybody's heard the story of Arthur and the sword IN the stone. But is the truth that Arthur fought in single combat, won, and took the sword ON the stone?

Of course, there are TWO Arthurs...

1 the warrior chief who may (or may not) have fought against the Saxon invasions of the 5th century and...

2 the King of legend who led the Knights of the Round Table into battles with dragons and giants and magic.

The trouble with Arthur 2 is that the stories always make Arthur out to be the greatest hero who ever lived. But an old saying goes, 'A man is never a hero to his personal servant.' He's probably not a hero to his wife either. Nobody ever bothers to tell Queen Guinevere's side of the story, do they? What would *she* have to say about her legendary husband?

Guinevere's grumble

A convent somewhere in Britain, 1815.

'I'll be back,' he said. I'm sure he will, but I've been waiting 1,300 years and he hasn't shown his miserable face yet. So where is he? That's what I want to know.

It was all so exciting back in AD 480. Most of the Romans had gone back to Italy but my family decided to stay. I was a noble Roman amongst all of the British peasants. I could have married anyone I wanted. But I admired those clever men who could write. And that was my downfall.

My father called me to his room one day. 'Ganhumara,' he said. 'How would you like to marry that famous Arthur?'

Well, I was so excited. I'd heard about the Saxon invaders and some British warriors fighting back. But I'd never heard of the famous Arthur.

I said, 'Oh, yes, father!' and rushed off to tell my sister.

Well, it wasn't till I got to church and saw all those nasty brutal men that I realized my mistake! He was the famous Arthur – so famous I'd never heard of him – and I thought father had said 'a famous author'! I've always been a trifle deaf.

My mistake. I had to make the most of it. First we moved into Arthur's hill fort. A filthy, draughty wooden castle he called Camelot – I always thought of it as Pong-a-lot! 'Who are you frightened of?' I asked him when I saw the place.

'I'm frightened of no one,' he said and went all huffy.

'Then why are you hiding in this castle?' I asked.

'I'm going to get a new army together to fight the Saxons,' he said.

'I'm not having hordes of sweaty soldiers tramping round

my clean floor, dripping blood all over those fresh rushes!'

'They're not sweaty soldiers. They're a better class. They're all knights, my lovely Guinevere,' Arthur said. He never could pronounce my Roman name. Guinevere, he called me, and the name stuck. There were a few names I'd like to have stuck on him but I decided to wait and see. And I was glad I did ... at first.

Some of those knights were really nice fellers. Galahad was always gadding about and Bedevere was a bit of a drip, but Lancelot was gorgeous. The trouble with those knights was that they were so proud. And once they'd beaten the Saxons they were bored. When knights have no one to argue with they argue with each other.

Arthur was the best fighter – ugly face, dirty fingernails and going bald – but the best fighter. Still, they weren't too happy about him being in charge.

'I sit at the top of the table with Guinevere,' Arthur demanded and there was a soft hiss of swords being drawn from belts. Arthur was as good as dead till I jumped up and said, 'Why don't you have a round table!'

They looked at me as if I was gormless. 'Tables is square,' Lancelot said. He was a lovely looking feller but he didn't have two brain cells to rub together.

'Arthur has carpenters in the castle. They can make a round table. Then there's no top of the table. Everybody's equal!' I cried.

'Sounds fair enough to me,' Galahad said and the others muttered in agreement.

We had a bit of trouble with the carpenter, of course. 'My saw doesn't cut circles,' he grumbled. 'It only cuts straight lines!' But, when Arthur told him his sword could cut a straight line across the man's throat, the carpenter went off and made one.

It was a bit wobbly on its legs but it did the job. That first feast night they had just eaten a couple of pigs and a deer when a servant rushed in with the bad news. 'Oh, my lords!' he cried. 'A terrible plague has swept the country and is killing the peasants. They're dropping like flies!'

'Well, I'm glad I'm not a peasant!' Arthur laughed.

'Or a fly!' Lancelot nodded.

'We have to help them!' the drippy Bedevere put in.

'Help them!' Arthur squawked. 'We're not Druids! We might catch something nasty!'

But Bedevere seemed to have a lot of support around the table. 'It's better than killing dragons,' Bedevere cried.

'Why?' I asked. 'I was always told that dragons are nasty scaly creatures with bad breath!'

'If we go on killing them at this rate there'll be none left in a hundred years! Dragons are becoming an endangered species!' Bedevere argued.

'Peasants will become an endangered species if you don't help them,' I said.

'Good thing,' Lancelot said.

'Lance, dear. If there are no peasants you'll have to dig in the fields and cut the corn and grind it to make flour and feed the pigs and shoe your horse ... everything,' I said.

'That's right. You'll have to do all that work yourself!' Bedevere argued.

Lancelot thought about this for a minute and his face was twisted with the effort. Finally he nodded. 'Save the peasants!' he cried and thumped the table. Of course he had to pick the spot with the wobbly leg. It took us ten minutes to pick up the wine and pig-meat off my clean rushes.

They decided that the only cure for the peasant plague was to drink from the Holy Grail – the goblet that Jesus drank from at the last supper. The trouble was nobody knew where it was.

'Why don't you have a quest?' I said quietly to Bedevere.

'Let's have a quest!' Bedevere said and his eyes went all starry. If there's one thing a knight likes it's a quest.

'It's a brilliant idea, Bedevere,' Arthur said.

'Thank you, Arthur,' Bedevere smiled.

I didn't mind. After all, it got those great clumping men out from under my feet.

Within a week they were packing their bags. 'Arthur,' I said in my sweetest voice. 'While you're away you'll need someone to run the country!'

'I've asked my nephew Mordred,' he said.

'I've never liked that shifty-eyed, weedy little cross-eyed brat,' I said. 'You should leave a trusty knight behind to keep an eye on him.'

Arthur nodded. 'I'll leave Lancelot,' he said.

'Perfect,' I said.

Now you've probably read the legends. But those stories about Lancelot and me are nothing but lies put about by that evil Mordred. Lance looked after me like a real gentleman. Maybe the odd cuddle when I got lonely but nothing more. Anyone else who says anything different is a liar. A liar like that Mordred.

The stories about his starting a rebellion were true though. Arthur dashed back from the quest and fought the devious little nephew at Camlann and beat him. Served the little traitor right.

The trouble is Arthur got a dreadful wound. The first I knew was Bedevere hammering on the gates. 'Come at once, Guinevere!' he cried. 'Arthur is close to death!'

'Close to deaf?' I said. 'I've always been a bit hard of hearing myself!' I laughed. 'Did I ever tell you that's how I came to marry him.'

'He's DYING!' Bedevere cried. 'He made me throw his sword Excalibur into the lake and a hand rose through the waters and took it below the surface. It's a sure sign death is close!'

I hurried to the scene of the battle and I got to my old feller just before he hopped the twig. That's when I heard those famous last words. 'I'll be back!' he croaked. 'Whenever Britain is threatened by the forces of dark and evil I will return and lead her to safety. I'll be back!'

And that was it. Lancelot went into a monastery and I went and became a nun. For 1,300 years I've waited. The Normans invaded and I thought that would bring him to Britain's rescue. Arthur slept through that and all the Middle Ages. In 1588 the Spanish Armada sailed to the attack … Arthur slept. Then in the 1800s a nasty Frenchman called Napoleon began rampaging across Europe and threatening to rule the world including poor little Britain.

Now, news is slow to reach this convent but I've just heard the news. Napoleon has been defeated by a British general at a battle in Belgium at a place called Waterloo. Our brilliant British general is known as the Duke of Wellington. He's a true British hero … just like my Arthur.

A nun brought me the news just now. 'What's the name of this British general?' I asked.

'The Duke of Wellington,' the girl replied.

'I know that. I mean the name he was christened with?'

'Oh!' the girl smiled. 'He's one of the Wellesley family, Sister Guinevere. I seem to remember his name is … Arthur. Yes, that's it. Arthur!'

I smiled and nodded. 'He said he'd be back.'

Now, Arthur Wellesley, Duke of Wellington, never claimed to be King Arthur reborn. But it's strange that our greatest general, the man who saved Britain when she was in mortal danger, should be called … Arthur.

The truth about Arthur

Over the centuries Arthur has become a British hero. Some people have built the most fantastic stories around him. They have said…

- Arthur was King of Atlantis – a kingdom that sank under the sea.

- Arthur was an alien who landed on Earth, zapped the Saxons then went off in his flying saucer.

- Arthur sailed west after his last battle and became the first European to discover America – a thousand years before Christopher Columbus.

The truth is…

1 If Arthur really existed then he lived in the 'Dark Ages' when no one was writing history. A couple of monks mentioned him. Nennius said…

> *At that time a great number of Saxons were invading Britain and increasing. Then Arthur and the British kings fought the Saxons. He was their battle leader. The pagans were put to flight that day and many of them were slaughtered. A twelfth battle took place at Mount Badon in which a single attack from Arthur killed 960 men. No other man took part in this massacre. In all these battles Arthur was the victor.*

2 The monk listed twelve battle sites and historians have argued about where they took place for a thousand years. No one really knows but it's fairly certain they were all over England, Wales and Scotland.

3 Historians argue over the line that says, 'No other man took part in this massacre' of 960 men! Most writers agree it means no other 'battle leader' took part in the massacre. If he killed 960 soldiers on his own then his little arms would be aching!

4 Arthur seems to have been the leader of some sort of travelling band of warriors. Tribal kings hired him to sort out the Saxons or pick on the Picts whenever trouble arose … but Arthur himself may not have been a king.

5 It was 600 years after his death that monks started writing histories about him and making him into the last of the Celt

super-heroes. Welsh monk, Geoffrey of Monmouth, wrote about Arthur in 1135, and added or invented or guessed at bits of Arthur's life. People believed they were 'facts' because they appeared in a history book! This is an important lesson. Never believe EVERYTHING you read in a history book! Geoffrey had the date of the last battle at Camlann as AD 542, by which time Arthur would have been 100 years old! No wonder the poor old wrinkly lost!

6 Then, in the 1150s, poems were written based on Geoffrey's 'facts' – Arthur's court at Camelot was invented in an 1180s' poem and the search for the Holy Grail was added in an 1190s' poem. Other storytellers added Merlin the magician, ladies in lakes and battles with evil knights.

7 In 1344 King Edward III of England got hold of the story and decided to have his own Knights of the Round Table. Then he changed his mind and the idea became the Knights of the Garter in 1348. Other kings of England or the United Kingdom have admired Arthur too. Henry VII named his son Arthur, Prince of Wales. But Arthur died before he came to the throne and his nasty little brother, Henry VIII, took over instead. The present Prince of Wales has Arthur as one of his middle names … and caused such a stir with

his marriage problems that some people said he should never be king. Are we doomed never to have a King Arthur? Is there a curse on the name?

8 A really large Round Table can be seen today in Winchester Castle and it is probably one of Henry III's bright ideas – it certainly isn't the real Arthur's Round Table.

9 Thomas Malory wrote a long poem called *The Death of Arthur* and it became one of the first books ever to be printed, in 1485. Arthur became a popular star and he still is today.

10 New films, books, plays, videos and magazines appear every year. There are coach trips to Arthur's sites, a King Arthur Society and you can even have a King Arthur holiday.

The truth is...

- There was almost certainly a strong and successful warrior among the Celtic Britons.
- For 30 years or more he held back the flood of Saxon invaders.
- When he died the Saxons invaded the country and the Celt Britons were finished.
- We don't know the name of this last great British Celt ... but we might as well call him ... Arthur.

Battlefield beliefs

As well as the Roman writers there were Celt poets who told tales of daring deeds. These too became a bit exaggerated. It was many years before these stories were written down and mistakes could have been made. For example, Celt Queen Boudicca was known for many years as Boadicea because of a monk's spelling mistake!

But the stories are interesting because there could well be truth behind them. In the legend of King Ailill Olomn's spear there are three things he mustn't do – he mustn't strike a stone, he mustn't kill a woman and he mustn't straighten the tip with his tooth. In fact, he kills a woman after she bites his ear. The spear goes through her and the tip buckles against a stone. He straightens it with his tooth … and is cursed. He goes blind, mad and (very strangely) develops bad breath. You'd think being blind and mad, having bad breath would be the least of his worries!

It's a fair guess that warriors straightened spear tips with their teeth but were warned not to. The warning became a little story – rather like Little Red Riding Hood is a warning not to talk to strange wolves in the wood.

Here are some of the other stories that Celts went into battle believing…

1 The Celts had Battle Furies to help them in war. These war-goddesses weren't actually fighters — more, frighters. The Nemhain (Frenzy), a charming goddess, had a powerful voice (like a dinner-lady telling you to line up properly). She shrieked at the Connacht army in Ulster and a hundred soldiers dropped dead with fright.

SHE'S THEIR SHRIEKRET WEAPON

2 The equally delightful Macha turned into a crow during a battle and hovered over the battlefield — she was waiting to make a meal of the heads of the dead fighters.

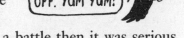

OOO! ANOTHER HEAD LOPPED OFF. YUM YUM!

3 If you saw the Badbh before a battle then it was serious bad news — she took the form of a crow, bleeding, with a rope around her neck. A sure sign that you are going to die. (If you see a bleeding crow before a football, hockey or netball match it is a sure sign that someone is going to lose! If the match is a draw

BLOOD STAINED ROPES ARE OK, BUT A RED TIE IS MORE COMFORTABLE

then you clearly made a mistake — you probably saw a crow that had been supping tomato sauce.)

4 On the other hand, Badbh was sometimes seen with a man. You could hardly miss him. He had one hand, one eye and one leg — he had a roast pig on his back which was still squealing. (Well, *you'd* be squealing if you'd been roasted.) If you see the bleeding hanged crow AND this feller hopping towards you it is probably time to get a tape measure and get measured for a coffin.

EEEEEEEE

HOW COME NOBODY WANTS TO BE FRIENDS WITH US?

5 But be careful if you see the Morrigan. She will urge you to fight and promise that you will win ... trouble is, she'll be saying exactly the same thing to the other side! Will you recognize the Morrigan? Possibly. She is red, with red hair and a red cloak, riding a chariot pulled by a red horse. In case you still don't spot her then take a close look at her horse ... it only has one leg, the chariot pole passes through its body and is fastened to its head with a peg. And I forgot to mention, her mouth is on the side of her face – a useful device for people who want to lick the wax out of one ear. (If you still can't spot her then you probably need to visit your optician.)

6 The Celts were fearless fighters yet they could easily be put off a fight. They believed that there were good days for fighting and bad days. There were signs that told a warrior to fight, or to pack up and go home. If he saw a crane bird, for example, he knew that would bring him bad luck. A crane would take away your courage and your skill – three cranes would leave you with as much fight as a lettuce leaf.

I'M *DEFINITELY* NOT FIGHTING TODAY!

Red was said by the Celts to be the colour of someone (or something) coming from the underworld. (This is not a reason to run away from pillar boxes, robins or Liverpool football players.)

How to be a hero
Celtic warriors enjoyed boasting about their victories. But they also liked to have little trophies that they could show to their friends. They were things to boast about. Here is a trophy that *you* can be proud of. To make it you will need a sharp sword, a wooden spoon and some lime (or cement).

1. Pick a fight with another hero. The more fierce he is then the greater the glory when you beat him *fig I*
2. Kill him (Please note: If he kills you then stop reading here) *see fig I*
3. Remove his head (Don't feel too bad about this. He'd do the same to you) *see fig II*
4. Remove the brain from the skull. *see fig III*
5. Mix the brain with lime to make a hard round ball
6. Show your prize at feasts and boast about your bravery

Here's one I made earlier!

57

This jolly little operation has its dangers – apart from the danger of your own brain ending up like a concrete football. The Celts believe that the brain can take its revenge, even after it's been removed.

Hero Conchobor killed Meisceadhra and made a trophy of his brain. But the brain was stolen and thrown at Conchobor. It hit him on the head … and stuck. For ever! In the end it drove Conchobor mad and he chopped oak trees down with his sword till he dropped dead.

Did you know … ?
The Celts did use brain power as well as muscle power sometimes. In 279 BC a Greek army broke down bridges to stop a Celt army pursuing them. The Celt land army had no boats but managed to cross the rivers by using their wooden shields as rafts. Clever Celts! Unfortunately they then went on to lose the battle, though they fought bravely – some warriors tore Greek spears out of their bodies and threw them back!

Potty prophetic hero
Place two fingers in your mouth and try speaking through them. This will not only allow you to spray your listeners with saliva, but also allow you to solve a mystery! The words you speak in this way will reveal some hidden truth.

But don't expect great things from this. The warrior

Fionn used the trick to detect the death of Lomna. He came across Lomna's body and said...

He has not been killed by a wild boar,
He has not been killed by a fall,
He has not died in his bed!

Amazing! How did he know all these things? Not really so very amazing. Lomna's body had no head on it. Even the British police could have guessed he did 'not die in his bed'!

Woe for women

Women in history are like the managers of football teams – they send their men out to battle with the weather or with the enemy. When they win the men get all the glory – when they lose the manager gets the sack … or the woman gets the blame. Celtic women had an equally difficult life…

- Women of the Parisii Tribe (now in East Yorkshire) were around 1.58 metres in height on average and most only lived to their early twenties. Giving birth to children was very dangerous and probably killed a lot of them.

- Celt women wore make-up made from juices of berries. Eyebrows were darkened with berry juice, a herb called ruam gave a red tint to cheeks and berry juice was used to redden the lips. The women also painted their nails. But a woman had to protect her eye shadow – the men liked to use it too!

- Women were proud of their long hair and carried their combs in a special comb-bag. Hair braids have been found in Ireland that are 1.5 metres long and even a warrior like Boudicca wore her hair to her knees.

But some things never change – it seemed Celt men preferred blondes. Both men and women wore golden balls plaited into the end of their hair and the men wore earrings too, as many do today. By this time you will have realized that the Celts loved their hair. The warriors bleached it with lime and arranged it into wild spikes. When a young man left home to become a warrior he had his hair cut to show that he was no longer a child.

- Large families shared a house – children lived with aunts and uncles and grandparents. Roman Julius Caesar said that groups of 10 to 12 men often shared wives. But the fact that the men shared the house doesn't mean they shared the women! No one can be sure.

- Graves have been discovered which show that some Celt women rose to become chiefs of their tribes. They were buried with battle chariots and weapons. Famous Macha of the Red Hair was said to rule all of Ireland and some historians believe she was a real person, not just a legend.

These warrior princesses were not the only women to be involved in war…

Ten things you never knew about fighting females
1 Irish landowners were expected to fight for their lord if he went to war. And if the landowner was a woman she was expected to fight. In the 6th century AD Saint Adamnan forced the law to be changed.
2 Women warriors in Irish tribes were teachers – but they didn't teach children to read and write. They trained the boys to fight. Do you know any women teachers like that?

THE TEST TOMORROW IS ON DISEMBOWELLING, SO STUDY YOUR SWORD SLASHES TONIGHT

3 Celtic women could be tribal chiefs and there was a woman army leader who led a group of Brigantian soldiers in an attack on the Romans some time between AD 71 and 83. Teuta led a Celtic tribe in the Mediterranean that took on the Greeks then the Romans. The Romans threatened to turn the whole of their army against her and sent a message warning her to behave. She had the messenger murdered! A huge Roman fleet forced her to make peace.
4 However, the more usual role of women was to spectate from carts and platforms at the back of the fighters and shout encouragement to their own fighters and insults or curses to the opposition – a bit like cheerleaders at American Football games. When the Gergovian Celts of Gaul lost to the Romans, the Celt women took all their clothes off in the hope that the Romans would spare them. Some hope!

5 Princess Canna was forced to marry Sinorix – King of the Storms – after he had murdered her husband. But it was a stormy marriage. One evening she offered Sinorix wine.

6 Women were not restricted to staying at home, teaching children, cooking or farming while the men went off to fight. Women in Gaul followed professions including wine-seller, butcher, doctor and chemist.

7 This may make women seem strong and powerful but Roman leader Julius Caesar said that in Gaul, men had the power of life or death over the women. He was probably wrong when he went on...

> *When the head of a noble family dies and there is some suspicion about the death, then his widow is questioned under torture. If she is found guilty of his death then she is sentenced to burn and sent to the flames with the most cruel torments.*

8 It's possible that women were Druid priestesses. Tacitus described the British forces which faced Suetonius Paulinus on Anglesey...

> *On the opposite shore stood the British army with its dense crowd of armed warriors. Between the columns dashed women in black gowns like the Goddesses of war, their hair wild, waving flaming torches. All around were the Druids, terrifying our soldiers.*

GULP GULP GULP

64

These women were also involved with human sacrifices. Tacitus said the Romans found the grisly remains of blood and guts on their altars in the woods.

9 Some also had the power of seeing into the future. Diocletian was a simple soldier in the Roman Army when he was paying his bill at a tavern. A Celtic woman approached him and said...

Years later Diocletian killed the Emperor's leading bodyguard and became Emperor – just as the woman had predicted. The name of the Emperor's bodyguard was 'Aper' ... a name meaning 'Boar'!

10 You can't always trust historians, of course. A Greek geographer called Strabo lived from about 40 BC till about AD 52 and he gave a description of priestesses living on an island off the coast of France. Many historians believe this island was Britain and the people by then would have been Celts. But would you have liked to pay a visit to their church? His report goes...

> *Posidonius says there is an island in the ocean, not far from land. The women there honour the god Dionysus and worship him with ceremonies and sacred rituals. It is their custom, once a year, to remove the roof from their temple and cover it again the same day before sunset. Each woman must carry part of the load. But if any woman lets her load drop then she is torn to pieces by the others. They then carry the pieces of her round the temple, chanting and do not stop till the madness passes away. But it always happens that somebody pushes against a woman who is chosen to suffer this fate!*

Imagine that! Being torn apart by a bunch of roofless women! Men were not allowed to land on the island. I can't imagine many men would want to!

Tall tales

And in the ancient Celtic stories naturally women are the villains. In Celt legends there are some strange women around.

1 In Irish legend Medb is cruel, jealous, unreliable and gets her power through witchcraft. In the end she was killed by the son of one of her victims. He killed her with a sling-shot like David killed Goliath ... but instead of a stone he hit her with a piece of cheese! (If it was soft cheese she'd be all right but if it was hard cheese then it was hard cheese for her.)

2 Boann made the mistake of visiting a well. Husband Nechtan was guardian of the well and told her not to go there. Nosey Boann had to have a look, didn't she? As a result the water gushed out of the well, drowned her and formed a river – now known as the Boyne in Eire. It's said

she's in there somewhere. If you ever go swimming in the Boyne and find a skeleton, you'll know who it is!

3 Rhiannon was accused of murdering her baby son. In fact it was pinched by an evil spirit but Rhiannon got the blame. Her ladies-in-waiting killed a puppy and smeared Rhiannon with blood as she slept. When she woke, covered in blood with no baby, her husband believed she had got rid of the baby's body ... by eating it!

4 A girl, Etain, was turned into a fly by a jealous goddess. This was quite useful because she could hum the god Midhir to sleep with her buzzing – or wake him up when danger came near. The jealous goddess was not satisfied and chased her so long and hard that Etain buzzed her way into a woman's wine glass. The woman drank the wine and swallowed Etain. (And before you ask, no, the woman did NOT swallow a spider to catch the fly, or swallow a bird to catch the spider that wriggled and wriggled and tickled inside her. That's another story altogether.) So anyway, next time you feel like swatting a fly, remember ... it could be some poor cursed girl!

True tale of terror

67

IN FACT SABINUS WAS HIDING IN A CAVE
HAH! FOOLED THEM. WHAT A CUNNING CELT I AM!
THEN EPONINA, HIS WIFE, JOINED HIM
THE ROMANS WILL BE WATCHING YOU. STAY AWAY
NO. I'LL ACT LIKE YOUR WIDOW BY DAY...
BUT EVERY NIGHT I WILL COME TO YOU
WHAT A COOL CELT IDEA!
FOR NINE YEARS THEY GOT AWAY WITH IT. BUT ONE DAY...
GOTCHA SABINUS. YOU'RE UNDER ARREST
OH CELTIC CURSES!
SABINUS WENT BEFORE THE EMPEROR
I SENTENCE YOU TO DEATH!
I PLEAD FOR MY LIFE!
GO AWAY YOU MISERABLE LITTLE PLEADER
AND YOU'RE A MISERABLE LITTLE CAESAR!

Eponina's wish had been to go to the Otherworld with her husband. She got her wish and they were executed that very day. Brave Celtic woman? Or a waste of a good life? What would you have done?

Cut-throat women
Some German tribes were closely related to the Celts. The Cimbrian holy women were a tough and bloodthirsty lot…

They were grey with age, wore white tunics and, over these, cloaks of the finest linen and bronze girdles. They were barefoot. These women would enter the camp of their warriors, sword in hand, and go up to the prisoners. They would then crown them and lead them up to a large bronze vessel. One of them would mount a step and, leaning over the cauldron, cut the throat of a prisoner who was held up over the vessel's rim. Others cut the body open and, after inspecting the entrails, would foretell victory for their countrymen.

You'll notice the women do not foretell the 'result' ... they foretell the 'victory'. In other words they know what the entrails (or guts) will say before they kill their victim! Seems like a waste of a good prisoner to be honest.

This story was told by Greek geographer Strabo and may have had some truth in it. However, do NOT try this at home. It makes a terrible mess on the carpet. If you want to look into the future then read your horoscope in the daily paper.

Cut-throat corpses

Women were also the victims of cut-throat carvers. In late Roman Britain there were many examples of people being buried with their heads removed and placed between their legs. Most of these were middle-aged or elderly women.

It's hard to say if they were beheaded before or after they were dead, but they were all beheaded very cleanly at the same neck bone and from the front. But why?

Some historians think it was so the women could see their way into the next life – a pair of eyes at your feet can come in very handy sometimes!

Or it could have been a punishment for witchcraft – many of these bodies have their jaws removed. That should shut them up in the next life all right.

Some women's heads are buried in wells – one in an Oxfordshire village called Headington (honest!).

Quaint Celt calendar

The Celts are an ancient people, older than the Ancient Greeks and maybe as old as the Ancient Egyptians. They built up a lot of traditions in that time. Quaint customs and events that were held at the same time every year. (A bit like school sports days at the end of term in July … followed by National Children's Gloom Day when everyone returns to school in the first week of September.)

When the Romans brought Christianity to the Celts then the Celts had many new customs to celebrate – saints' days, Christmas and Easter, for example. But they never forgot the old customs and the old gods. The Celt calendar became a mixture of Christian and non-Christian.

If you want to remember the cut-throat Celt calendar then here are a few diary dates for you…

Deidre's Diary

November
1st. Dear Diary. Here we go again. Another New Year's Day and the first day of winter. Old goddess Cailleach has hit the ground with her hammer and made it hard. I know it's true. I have to sleep on it. And this is my first winter married to that dear lump-head Fionn. This is also the day when the village Druid makes sacrifices to all the gods. I'll bet the Druid eats the goat himself. I think that's why he's so fat. My friend Rhiann says she saw him chewing on a goat bone. Of course we daren't say anything – we might end up on the altar instead of the goat!
9th. Time to bring the cattle in for the winter – dead or alive. Of course I get the job of killing and salting the feeble cows and sheep. I wouldn't mind but I'll get blood all over this new diary

December

18th. This is the day of the Goddess Epona, you know, the one who looks like a horse. My friend Rhiann says her sister looks like Epona but I think that's a bit cruel — horses are much better looking than Rhiann's sister! Anyway, today is the day when horses and donkeys have a day of rest. I wish I did. Work, work, work. And that lump-head husband is as much use as the icicle on the end of me nose.

21st. Longest night of the year. We light fires for the warmth and the light but the lump-head Fionne brought in damp wood and the smoke almost choked us and the pig. I said to the lump-head, "If I want smoked bacon I'll kill the pig and hang it over the fire... but I don't!"

January

25th. Dwynwen's day. This is the day when lovers give tokens to their loved ones. What did I get from that lump-head? The whole contents of his head: nothing. But my friend Rhiann says young Gildas would like to give me his heart. I'd rather have a fresh piece piece of pork.

31st. Feast of Oimelc. Usual over-eating and over-drinking to celebrate winter loosening its grip. Not that you'd notice. Water in the buckets still frozen. Fionn has an excuse for not washing his feet. This is the time when the old Hag of Winter, Cailleach, sends her Dragon to kill Brigit of Spring. If Brigit loses then it will be winter forever! Every year Brigit sends a lamb to fight the dragon and it always wins. Must be a tough lamb – tough as the sheep we stewed and ate last night. I wish Spring would come with its fresh meat – and fresh air.

February

1st. Ogronios – the time of ice. My friend Rhiann says that today the women of Gaul stain their bodies blue with woad and march naked through the village! At this time of year! Lumphead Fionn said I should take all my clothes off. I gave him such a smack!

14th. Rhiann's sister gave birth to a baby boy today. I was there and took part in the blessing. We passed the baby three times across the fire, then we carried it three times around the fire – sunwise, of course. Rhiann filled a bowl with water & and the Druid dropped a gold coin in it. The baby was washed in the golden water. The little beggar didn't like it one bit. Still, judging by the screams he has healthy enough lungs! Whining about being washed in a drop of cold water — just like a man — just like smelly Fionn.

March

21st. Alban Eiler day when the days begin to grow longer than the nights. The men go out hunting to celebrate and the women watch. My friend Rhiann's father caught a deer and even my stupid brother caught a rabbit. What did lump-head Fionn catch? A cold. Tonight we'll be eating porridge again.

April

30th. Beltain eve. At last! We can open the doors in the village wall and let the cattle out to graze. The smell has been appalling in the past few weeks. What with the cattle dung and Fionn's feet I thought I was going to choke some nights. We drove the cattle between the bonfires to purify them. Fionn got drunk and I wondered if I should purify him by pushing him onto one of the bonfires. Decided not. It'll soon be Beltain and then we'll see.

May

1st. Beltain and the first day of summer.
That's it! Went to the village druid and asked
for a divorce from Fionn. He tried to tell me that
smelly feet is not a good enough reason for
divorce... then he smelled Fionn's feet. I'm free.
Good idea this trial marriage over winter. Three
other women of the village got divorced today.
When Fionn sobers up after last night's feast I'll tell
him he's divorced then throw him out of the house.

June

20th. Midsummer's Eve. Tonight my friend
Rhiann and me went out gathering yarrow. We
chanted the old rhyme:

Good morrow, good yarrow, good morrow to thee
    Send me this night my true love to see.
The clothes he will wear and the colour of hair
    And tell me if he will wed me.

Then we put the yarrow under our pillow
and waited for our love
to appear in our dream.
Rhiann dreamed about
young Colum. I dreamed
about tucking into a leg of
fresh pork

yarrow

21st. The longest day. My friend Rhiann and me stayed up tonight for a death-watch. They do say that we see the ~~spirit~~ spirits of those who'll die before the end of the year! I thought I saw the naked body of my lump-head husband but it was only a pig in the moon light. What a shock!

July 14th. This is the day when we make wishes at the well. Me and Rhiann dipped our strips of cloth in the magic water and hung them out to dry on a hawthorn bush. As they hang there and dry the wish starts to come true. I can't tell my wish or it will not come true. But it did have something to do with food. After all, July is called the Hungry Month — all of last year's grain is gone and this year's hasn't ripened. And I know Rhiann wished she could marry Colum.

31st. Feast of Lughnasadh. This is the time when women choose husbands — and sometimes the husbands get to choose a wife. If they want a trial marriage then they join hands through a magic stone with a hole in the middle. Colum joined hands with Mara and Rhiann was very upset. Tore her wishing cloth off the

thorn bush! I think I'll give it a miss this year.
The hay's been gathered in but there's still the
wheat and barley to gather. At least the
Lughnasadh horse fair and the horse races
give us a break.

August

6th. We had a trial in the village today. A
sheep had gone missing and Ogma was found
with a pot full of stewed mutton. First he said
it was his own sheep but then the druid counted
Ogma's sheep and found they were all there. So
the druid held a trial in the middle of the
village. He said there were three stones in his
bag; he would draw one out. Black for guilt,
white for innocence and speckled for partly
guilty. The druid pulled out the speckled stone.
Ogma admitted he was partly guilty – he didn't
steal the sheep but he did find it dead and
didn't tell the owner. The druid said the gods
would punish Ogma.

8th. The gods are right again! Ogma has
died. That sheep he found was diseased. When
he ate the meat it made him ill and killed
him. No one will ever steal a dead sheep in
this village again. I can tell you!

September

21st. Nights become longer than days again. This is the time when I'm wishing I had a man of my own. Fionn wasn't much good but at least he kept me warm in the long cold nights.

24th. A poet came to the village today and sang a ballad about a pair of lovers, Baile and Ailinn. Baile heard Ailinn was dead so he killed himself. Ailinn heard that Baile was dead so she killed herself. Even when they were dead they went and buried them in separate graves. I thought it was a waste of two lives, myself, but my friend Rhiann started blubbering. You'd never catch me crying. Well not in front of the other villagers, though my eyes were watering a little when I ~~went~~ got into my lonely bed.

October

31st. Samhain eve. Ooooh! This is the night when the spirits of the dead wander the world. Rhiann says my dad will come back and visit me. But, since he was cut to bits in a battle with the Picts I don't really want to see him in pieces! Then Rhiann told me a ghost story and scared the hair half off my head. One Samhain eve a young man called

Nera accepted a challenge. There were two corpses hanging from a gallows on the hilltop. Nera agreed to tie a grass rope round the foot of one corpse for a bet. But as soon as the rope touched the foot Nera vanished into the Otherworld and was never seen in this world again! I wonder ~~was~~ what the new year will bring for me and Rhiann?

Did you know … ?

From the ancient laws of Hywel Dda we know that medieval Welsh kings had a servant known as a 'Foot Holder'. Believe it or not the Foot Holder held the king's feet! From the time the king sat down to eat his evening meal, the Foot Holder took the king's feet in his lap and held them till he went to bed. While the king's feet were off his kingdom he could relax – he wasn't king for a while. The Foot Holder had the power; criminals could ask the Foot Holder for a pardon and he would probably allow them to go free – the king would have had to punish them.

Crazy Celt life

The Celts were farmers — when they weren't hunting animals or fighting Romans. They kept cows and sheep and hens and so on. Sounds idyllic, doesn't it? But would you like to have lived as a Celt? Read the facts and make up your own mind...

1 The Celts dressed to keep warm but they also liked to put on a bit of a show. Women wore checked skirts and when they went to important meetings they wore make-up, bracelets, anklets, necklaces, finger-rings, earrings and hairpins. Richer women also wore the gold neck bands (torques) that were worn by hero warriors. The Celts had no buttons — they used pins or brooches and those pins would be decorated too. Imagine having decorations on your zips!

2 Irish Celts seem to have been very clean people. They washed hands and feet every morning and had a full bath every night. They scrubbed themselves with soap and a linen cloth. The good news is that the water was usually

heated. The bad news is you'd probably share that water with the rest of the family.

3 The Celt houses were made of wattle walls – thin branches 'woven' to make panels which were then plastered with mud to keep the draughts out. The roofs were thatched and the fire built in the middle of the single large room that everyone shared. The trouble is there does not seem to have been a chimney for the smoke to escape. Sparks must have caused a lot of roof fires and the smoking would definitely be bad for your health!

4 The Celts built these houses in groups – often on the top of a hill and often with a defence wall around them. You'd call it a hill fort or a village, because you are sensible. But a horrible historian show-off would call it an 'oppidum'. You do not really need to know this … but if you ever get bored on a car journey then, every time you pass a village, you can sing, 'Oppidum, oppidum, oppidum-dum-dum!' till everyone in the car is driven mad.

5 Clean fingernails were a must. If someone damaged your fingernail they had to pay you for the damage under Irish law. A great Irish insult was to call a man 'Ragged nails!'

6 They probably used iron bars as a sort of money. They'd swap the 80 cm bars for other goods. Anyone with a dirty great magnet could have made a fortune as a pick-pocket!

7 The Celts had another useful type of money. You didn't have to carry it round with you ... it walked! It was called a slave. These slaves could be people captured in battle or defeated during an invasion. The Romans used slaves and made wine – the Celts enjoyed wine but lived too far north to grow grapes. So the Celts swapped slaves for wine. WARNING: Do not let your parents know this or they may take you to the local off-licence and try to trade you for a can of lager.

8 The Celts ate off plates made of pottery, but sometimes the plates were made of wood...

THIS FOOD TASTES BURNT

NO. THE PLATE'S MADE OF ASH

The Celts ate with their fingers, and a fussy Roman wrote...

They eat cleanly but like lions, raising up whole limbs with both hands and biting off the meat.

CHOMP CHOMP

9 Celts had very little furniture so they slept on the floor wrapped in animal skins – bearskin or wolfskin kept you warm. Of course, you could end up even warmer running away from the bears and wolves as you tried to nick their skins!

10 The Celts were very fond of hunting. It got rid of pests (like deer that ate their crops), provided them with food (like wild boar) and clothing (wolfskin) but above all it gave them a popular form of entertainment. They used long-handled spears, bows and metal-tipped arrows or sling shots. These weapons need a lot of practice. If you don't believe me then make one and pop off to your nearest forest. I'll bet you don't kill a single wolf or bear if you hunt all year. (No going to a zoo to win this bet! Zoos is cheating!)

Live like a Celt

If you hopped on a time machine and were dropped in a Celt settlement then would you survive? Try this quick quiz. Get all the questions right and you'll fit in well with the Celts. Get one wrong and they may suspect you are not one of them. You'll end up with something at your throat – if you're lucky it may be a slave chain – if you're unlucky it may be a Druid's sacrificial knife!

1 The Celts loved a good party. The wine or beer is passed around. As a special guest you can drink first. But how should you drink the wine?

a) Empty your goblet in one swallow.

b) Refuse the drink until the chief has drunk first. (You could say, 'Thanks but I'd rather have a Coke.')

c) Drink a small sip then pass the goblet on.

2 As the party goes on a warrior stands up and tells everyone how he bravely fought against ten Roman soldiers

and beat all of them. Everyone looks at you. What do you say?

a) 'Liar! Liar! Pants on fire.'

b) 'You are a brave and noble warrior. I believe you and praise your courage.'

c) 'That's nothing, mate. I beat 20 Roman soldiers; I had one hand tied behind my back, I was wearing a blindfold and the only weapon I had was a sharp fingernail.'

3 A wild boar has been roasted for the party. You are offered a trotter to chew on. What do you say?

a) 'Thank you, that is extremely kind of you.'

b) 'I hope you've checked this boar for mad pig disease! Anyway, I'm a vegetarian and I'd prefer a nut cutlet.'

c) 'I will eat nothing but the best meat. Give me the finest flesh or you will die and I'll be roasting you on the fire.'

4 The tribe explains that this is the feast of Beltain. A ceremony is about to take place. Two large bonfires are lit.

The warriors ask if you know what happens next. What do you say?

a) 'I guess we pop Guy Fawkes on top of one fire then set off the fireworks!'

b) 'We take it in turns to plunge a hand into the fire to show our courage.'

c) 'We drive the cattle between the two fires and this will protect them from disease.'

5 The Druid is a kind old bloke in a long, hooded robe. He says he has a special drink for a noble guest like you. It is made from the juice of the mistletoe. What do you do?

a) Drink it.

b) Offer to share it with the Druid.

c) Refuse to drink it. Make some excuse, like you were

always taught to 'Say NO to a stranger …' and they don't come much stranger than the Druid!

6 The Druid suggests that it would be good to make an offering to the goddess, Sulis. She will bless the tribe in the coming battles. You go down to the river – everyone knows Sulis lives in water. You are given a fine knife with a gold pattern on the handle. What should you do with it?

a) Cut your hand and let a little blood drip into the river.

b) Throw the knife into the river as a rich gift.

c) Throw the knife into the river – but break it first so Sulis doesn't cut herself.

Answers:

All 'c)' answers are correct. If you have just one 'a)' or 'b)' you would not fit in with the Celt ways and probably not survive, either. That could be your ticket to the Otherworld! Here's why...

1 The Celts drank small sips ... but drank an awful lot of those small sips until they were very drunk!

2 Warriors took part in Boasting Contests. No one ever called anyone a liar but a lot of exaggerating went on and that was all part of the enjoyment.

3 The bravest warriors expected the best meat. Only a wimp would make do with less. Being given a bone is an insult – accept it and you're a wimp. Start a fight if necessary to get the best.

4 Cattle were kept inside the village fence all winter. At the beginning of May they were driven out onto the grass meadows for summer grazing. The fires represented the warming and life-giving sun and the Druids drove the cattle between two fires to protect them from evil. Other big days included 1 February, known as Imbolc – the start of the lambing season – plenty of ewes milk for cheese. 31 July was Lughnasadh, when crops were ripening and a party for the gods would make sure they were safely gathered in.

5 A Roman historian called Pliny said, 'The Celts believe that the mistletoe, taken in a drink, is a cure for all poisons.' But the truth is that Druids must have known that mistletoe is in fact a poison – they gave it to sacrificial victims. Maybe it knocked them unconscious so they wouldn't struggle so much when the Druids cut their throats!

6 The Celts always broke or bent a knife before offering it to Sulis. They also threw their most valuable possessions into the rivers, including solid gold cups. But if Sulis lived in water, what would she want with a cup?

Did you know … ?

The Celts grew grain and when they had spent all year growing the stuff they put most of it in a hole in the ground. This is not because they were crazy Celts, but because a hole in the ground would keep it fresh until they were ready to grind it into flour.

Flour was made by placing grain on a large flat stone called a quern – then rubbing a stone over the grain. It took 90 minutes to make a kilo of flour. After the 2nd century BC a rotary quern was invented and a kilo of flour took just 10 minutes to produce.

The grain pits were also used to dump dog or horse sacrifices. Imagine opening your flour bag from the supermarket and finding a bit of dead dog. You'd probably never eat bread again!

If you want a taste of Celtic life then try these recipes…

Pease pudding

You need:

250g dried green peas
pinch of mint herb
pinch of thyme herb
25g butter
half a teaspoonful of salt

Method:

1 Soak the dried peas for 12 hours (overnight is best).

2 Put the peas and the herbs in a saucepan and boil them in half a litre of water for half an hour. They should be soft and the skins loose.

3 Pour them into a sieve to let the water drain away, then use a spoon to force the peas through the sieve, giving a pea paste. (If you're really lazy then use a blender. Celts did not have blenders.)

4 Stir in the butter and salt then place the mixture in a greased pudding basin. Cover it with foil (which the Celts didn't have) and put the basin in a covered pan of boiling water. Boil it for an hour, but don't let it boil dry. WARNING: Puddings boiled in this way have a nasty habit of giving the cook third-degree burns. Get an adult to do this for you (so they get the burns, while you get to eat the pudding).

5 Take the foil off the basin, put a plate over the

top and turn the plate and the basin upside down. If you're lucky the pease pudding will come out in a neat, basin-shaped lump. (If you're unlucky it will come out as a slimy green mess, but eat it anyway.)

Porridge
You need:

50g oatmeal
600ml water
pinch of salt
milk

Method:

1 Boil the water in a saucepan and add the salt.
2 Sprinkle in the oatmeal a little at a time and stir each time you add some.
3 Boil for 20 minutes.
4 Serve in bowls and stir in some milk.
5 If you prefer it sweet then stir in a spoonful of honey – the Celts didn't have sugar.

(This may taste quite pleasant, but most Celts ate it every day and you could soon become sick of it!)

Awesome animals

It was a hard life being a Celt, dodging the Druids and running from the Romans. But it was worse for the animals. The Celts were very close to nature and they told remarkable tales about animals. They also had some strange beliefs about them. Believe these stories if you want...

Deer

- Cernunnos was Lord of All the Stags and appeared as a man with antlers. It is very useful to walk around with a coat rack on your head but it's murder when you want to wash your hair in the sink.

- Irish Prince Tathan landed in Wales to set up a monastery. As his crew threw a rope to the shore a stag stepped forward and put a hoof on the rope to prevent the ship drifting away. Tathan went off to teach the wild Welsh about Christianity.
- When Tathan and his friends returned to the ship they were weak from hunger. Nobody had so much as a bag of crisps (well, they hadn't been invented, had they?). But the stag came to the rescue yet again. 'Eat me,' he said. So they did. Stag steak is very tasty they reckon, especially with mushy peas and chips.

Pigs

The Celts believed that pigs (and sows in particular) were very wise. It made sense to listen to what a pig had to say. There are lots of tales about swine-herds who turn out to be Princes in disguise. If you wanted to get a head, get a pig.

- St Brannoc set up a church where he found a sow with her piglets – a dream told him to do this.
- A boar appears on many Celtic coins (where now we have the queen's head – no comments please about bores or pigs or you could end up in the Tower of London).
- The Goddess of Hunting, Archinna, is usually pictured riding a boar with a dagger in her hand. She is clearly into pork chops.

Wrens

- The Celts told a story about a competition for the king of the birds. The eagle flew highest and claimed to be king. But a wren had hitched a ride on the eagle's back and flew still higher. The wren was king of the birds.
- Wrens had a tough time at New Year. They were killed because the Celts believed that it was a way of saying goodbye to the old year and bringing luck to the new. It was not, of course, very lucky for a wren.

- Sailors until recently still believed that the feather of a wren protected them from drowning, especially if the wren was killed on New Year's Day. This led to the mass slaughter of wrens in the old Celt kingdom, the Isle of Man, because the sailors' protection only lasted one year.

Dogs

- Dogs were respected in Celtic life. They were useful for hunting, and they also protected their owners.
- The lick of a dog was supposed to heal a wound. WARNING: Never, ever, try this even if your dog has just gargled with antiseptic!
- The God of the Underworld had a pack of white dogs with red ears. If you ever see such a dog you can tell it to go to Hell, because that's just telling it to go home!
- Druids may have respected dogs but this didn't stop them from chewing dog flesh for mystic power.

Miserable medicine

- Celt doctors bored into a patient's skull to relieve pressure on the brain. This was particularly useful if your skull had been bashed in battle.
- The Celts also believed in the healing powers of water. The Romans are famous for their healing waters at England's west-country city of Bath. But the Celts discovered it before the Romans got there and were using the waters long after the Romans had gone. The waters probably helped with some illnesses but the Celts believed it was the Goddess, Sulis, who really healed them.

- The Romans taught the Celts the trick of writing your problem on a thin piece of lead, rolling it up and dropping it into the water. (This is a bit like taking a prescription from the doctor and giving it to the chemist. The difference is we can read the lead inscriptions even today – the handwriting of doctors is impossible to read!) No one worried if they couldn't write. They simply made a little model of their poorly parts and dropped it in the water!
- While you were at the Bath waters – drinking it and bathing in it – there were doctors hanging around who offered to cure you if the waters didn't work. And, while you were there, you could also take the time to curse somebody who had upset you. A lot of curse messages have been found. They said things like...

Did you know ... ?
To protect yourself against illness you should take your middle two fingers, place them in your mouth and spread them. This 9th century Celtic charm against illness only works if you've washed your hands first, of course ... especially if you've just had them up your nose.

Celtic life – test your teacher

1 What did the Celts put on their ponies to protect them during races?

a) Shin guards (like footballers wear) made of whale bones.

b) Crash-helmets made of metal.

c) Leather boots cushioned with sheepskin.

2 How did Bronze-Age Scots try to strengthen their fortress walls to keep the Celts out?

a) They cemented the stones together.

b) They nailed the stones together.

c) They set huge bonfires against the wall to melt the stones together.

3 Some Celts got away with a debt in a curious way. What did they say to someone they owed money to?

a) 'I'll pay you in the next life.'

b) 'I'll toss a coin with you – double or quits.'

c) 'You can have my wife instead of the money.'

I SUPPOSE WE COULD TOSS YOUR WIFE INTO THE NEXT LIFE, DOUBLE OR QUITS

4 The Pict tribes of Scotland knew about it, but modern Brits only found it in 1933. What?

a) Celtic football team.

b) Invisible ink.

c) The Loch Ness Monster.

5 St Cybi was a brilliant child. A writer said this incredible child could do what at the age of just seven years?

a) Read a book.

b) Sacrifice a goat.

c) Learn the Bible and recite it from memory.

6 Skeletons of Celt women have been found buried with their rings. But where were they wearing them?

a) On their fingers.

b) On their toes.

c) In their noses.

7 When the Celts became Christian you could still spot the difference between their monks and the Roman monks. How?

a) They wore blue robes dyed in woad.

b) They shaved their heads from ear to ear, not in a neat circle.

c) They chanted their songs in the Gaelic language, not Latin.

8 Where did the Picts get their name from?

a) They were the chosen people of the gods – the Picked or Pict.

b) The first iron tools they made were stone-breakers called 'Picks'.

c) The Romans thought they were like 'Pictures' because they painted themselves.

9 If you killed a child under the age of seven, what would be your punishment?

a) You would be fined three cows.

b) You would be hanged.

c) You would have the hand that did the killing cut off.

10 Historians argue about exactly who King Arthur was. One thing's for certain. Arthur was not his proper name – just a nickname. What does 'Arthur' mean?

a) He who fights on two sides.

b) Great leader of 100 battles.

c) Bear.

Answers:

1 b) Pony caps, with holes for the ears, have been found at Celtic sites in the Shetlands. But what on earth were they doing to need this sort of head protector? Pony-American-Football?

2 c) The Bronze-Age Celts of Scotland created these 'vitrified forts' where the stones were heated till they were 'welded' together. One can be seen at Craig Phadrig near Inverness. Don't try this on your house – bricks don't melt.

3 a) This worked for Celts who believed they were getting a good deal if they could collect money in the Otherworld. If you really want to persuade someone that you can be trusted then take the Celtic Curse:

If I break my promise may the skies fall upon me, may the seas drown me and may the earth rise up and swallow me!

However, the bad news is that modern Celt shopkeepers don't believe this line and will not give you a bar of chocolate or a mountain bike if you promise to pay in the next life. Sorry.

99

4 c) The Picts carved pictures on stones, and one stone stands at Aberlemno village between Forfar and Brechin. It shows a long-nosed swimming creature like an elephant – except its trunk comes from between its ears. This ties in with the Celtic legend of St Columba (AD 521 – 597) who tamed such a monster in Loch Ness. Another monk was less lucky – he let the lake monster plough his field for him. When the job was finished the monster vanished ... taking the monk with him!

5 a) Cybi could read. This might not amaze you as much as it amazed the monk who wrote his life story, but being able to read was very rare in the 6th century. If you can read this then you probably could read at seven. Why not go home and tell your parents, 'Did you know I could be a Saint? I really think that means you should double my pocket money.'

6 b) There wouldn't have been much point in wearing a ring under your shoes – no one would see your jewellery and it would be uncomfortable. No Celtic shoes have ever been found so the toe-rings suggest that women often wore sandals.

7 b) They shaved their heads from ear to ear but sometimes the Celt monks left a tuft of hair at the top of the head. A Saxon monk called Bede (who shaved a round bald patch) thought they looked a bit ridiculous.  Maybe he should have looked in a mirror! Some historians think the Celt monks may have copied the Druids in this hair fashion. Celt monks also amazed the Europeans by wearing black eye make-up – a fashion they kept from Celt warriors.

8 c) The Picts were nicknamed 'Picture People' by the Romans but their real name was Cruitne. The Picts lived in Scotland where they were joined by the Scots who came from Ireland. In time there were more Scots than Picts so Pictland became Scotland. Got it? It could be worse – the Britons called them Priteni. Edinburgh could now be the capital of Priteniland. Try spelling that in a geography lesson some wet Wednesday.

9 a) A child under seven was considered to be worth as much as a priest! Any child under 14 could not commit a crime – the parents had to take the blame. This hasn't changed much 2,000 years later. If you skip school then your parents end up with a fine.

10 c) 'Arthur' meant 'Bear'. The other two nicknames are from the Dark, or Middle, Ages. Celt leader Vercingetorix meant 'Great leader of 100 battles' while a leader in Gaul was named Ambigatus meaning 'He who fights on two sides' ... which is a funny thing to do. If he was fighting on both sides he'd have to try to kill himself while at the same time try to stop himself being killed by himself. He could end up in more knots than a boy scout's tent-rope.

Cheerless children

You think school is bad? You'd probably prefer it to being a Celtic child. All work and very little play. From the time you could walk you'd be given jobs like weeding the fields, combing the wool ... and watching the fleas and lice jump out onto you as you comb. (That should keep you up to scratch!)

Sets of coloured glass counters, a little like modern marbles, have been found at Celtic sites. They seem to be from some board game a bit like Ludo. Unfortunately the

Celts were not great writers so there's no rule book with the counters and no one knows how the game was played.

Simple games *have* survived from the period and here's one you can try...

Knife-cloth-stone
You'll need:
• two players, preferably with at least one hand each.
All you do is:
1 On the count of three each player brings a hand out from behind their back. They have made a shape with that hand.
• A pointing finger is a knife.
• A spread hand is a cloth.
• A tight fist is a stone.
2 The winner is the one whose object can destroy the other player's. So...
• A knife beats a cloth because it can cut it.
• A stone beats a knife because it can blunt it.
• A cloth beats a stone because it can wrap around it.
3 A point is scored every time a player wins. The first to score 10 is the winner.

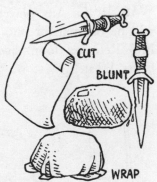

Hurley
The Irish have a rough form of hockey known to the Celts as 'hurley', and in modern Irish as 'hurling'.
You'll need:
• two teams of 15 players each with a hurling stick – like a hockey stick with a broad end

- two goals (like five-a-side soccer goals with extended uprights to make an 'H' shape)
- a hard ball like a rounders ball.

All you do is:

1 The aim is to score a 'Goal' – three points if it goes under the crossbar, one point over the crossbar but between the posts.

2 Play like hockey – except you can carry the ball on the hurling stick for as far as you want and you can catch the ball in the hand, but...

3 You can't pick up the ball from the ground in the hand, throw the ball or run with it in the hand more than two strides.

4 Horrible hurling: you are not allowed to use your stick to batter or trip an opponent ... but ancient warriors are said to have played this game with the head of an enemy. WARNING: Any player trying to play with a head today will be banned for one game (and probably locked up for life). Referees do not accept the excuse, 'But the cut-throat Celts did it.'

ARE WE WINNING?

WE'RE JUST A HEAD

Baile

This game is a bit like team-golf.

You'll need:

- four or more players, each with a hockey stick and a ball
- a hole in the ground about a metre wide. (This may be difficult to dig in your school playground. A chalk circle may have to do!)

All you do is:

1 The aim is to hit the hole (or target circle) with a ball.

2 One player is the goalkeeper. He or she plays against the rest.

3 The team form a line facing the hole, at least 10 metres away. (This can be altered to more, or less, as you learn the game and want to make it more even.)

4 Team players strike a ball, one at a time, and try to hit the target. The goalkeeper tries to stop a ball hitting the target.

5 When everyone on the team has had a shot at the target then the score is counted – one point for a hit.

6 The team then defends the target while the goalkeeper takes a shot with each ball and tries to score more than the team.

WHAP!

A HOLE IN ONE

Note 1: A Celt story describes one boy playing in goal against 150 – he stopped every ball. When it was his turn to shoot he scored with every one of his 150 shots! As a modern hockey player he would be wanted by every team in the world!

Note 2: Pottery images of this game show that the players wore no clothes. You could try this if you wanted but you might be arrested by the police, who are not trained to understand Celtic laws.

Note 3: The images also appear to show the game being played with a head instead of a ball. You probably wouldn't want to use a head in your school yard because heads don't bounce as well as tennis balls. They just sort of hit the ground and go 'splatt!'

Did you know ... ?

- Boys and girls in Celt Ireland were sent away from home as soon as they were old enough – probably about seven. They went to live with a family in a neighbouring tribe. This taught them they belonged to the whole tribe and not just one father and mother. They stayed there until they were about 17 years old.
- The boys were not taught how to fight by the tribe's champion – he'd be far too busy. Instead they were often taught by women warriors.
- Girls married at the age of 12 to 14 and until then would be said to be 'beside her father's plate'.

Crime and punishment

The Celts may have seemed wild and lawless to the Romans but in fact they had their own type of law and order. The Druids took on special jobs. Some advised the people or the king, some acted as priests, some as fortune-tellers and some as judges. The judge-Druids were known as Brehons.

A Brehon settled arguments, listened to complaints and decided if there was a crime. The Brehon could also order punishments if he or she thought someone was guilty.

Trial by the gods

The Brehons could not always be sure of someone's guilt. There were no video surveillance cameras, no fingerprints, no blood tests and none of the scientific tests that today's police have. But the Brehons believed they had something better. A god who has seen everything!

All they had to do was leave the decision to chance – the god would make sure that chance pointed out the right victim. Why not try it and see if it works?

Casting the woods

This system was used by Druids in murder trials ... but we don't really want to murder someone just to test it ... no, not even the class bully deserves that.

You'll need:

- three people – one Brehon Judge, two suspects
- three pieces of wood – sticks from ice lollies would be perfect. (Yes, I know the Celts didn't have ice lollies – stop trying to be so clever and just get on with the trial, will you?) You will also need something to scratch words onto the sticks and a bag or hat to hide the sticks in.

All you do is:

1 Place a valuable object on a table – a watch, a jelly baby, the crown jewels ... anything.

2 The Brehon turns his or her back.

3 One of the suspects steals the valuable object and hides it on their person.

4 The Brehon then holds the 'casting-the-woods' trial...

- If the Celt farmers discovered someone's animal had damaged a fence then who had the job of fixing the fence? The animal's owner, since cattle aren't very handy with a hammer. How will they decide whose beast did the damage? By casting the woods.

- And if a Celt accidentally hurt a bee then he had to pay the owner of the hive for the loss. Everyone had bees and hives. How did they know which hive the bee came from? No, they didn't have little rings around their bees' knees like pigeons. The Celts would cast the woods.

Why can't we just do this today? Two cars crash – who's to blame? Cast the woods! Two soccer teams are level after extra time in a cup match. Who goes on to the next round? Cast the woods! You need £5 to go to the cinema. Who should pay? Cast the woods – just make sure each wood has the letters D-A-D scratched on it!

Did you know … ?

Sometimes a Druid Judge decided that a whole family was to blame for the crime of one person. This would be a bit like your brother breaking a window … but the cost of repairing it is taken from your pocket money!

Make the punishment fit the crime

Here are five Celt crimes … if you were a judge, what would *you* do to the criminal found guilty?

CRIME

1 deserting your tribe in battle

2 Calling a woman ugly

3 killing a woman who has run off with your husband

4 Burning a building down

5 Violent crime

Punishment

A fined

B Exile

C Hanged from a tree

D Death by drowning

E no punishment

Answers:

1 c) Traitors and deserters were hanged from trees. Trees were particularly important to Celts because they were like a picture of life – roots in the underworld and branches in this world. Hanging sent a man straight to the Otherworld!

2 a) You were fined for insulting a woman's appearance, making up a nickname for them, making fun of some weakness they had or for telling an untrue story about them.

3 e) A woman who killed her husband's girlfriend could get her revenge in any way she wanted … so long as she did it within three days of finding out about them. After three days she should have calmed down – any action then becomes a crime.

4 b) Celts believed that their land went as far as the ninth wave from the shore. Exiled criminals were set adrift with no oars or sail or steering paddle. They were given just a knife and some fresh water and left to the mercy of the gods. They usually died, but if they were swept back to the shore they became a slave.

In legends there were saints and heroes who survived this punishment and went on to do great deeds. In the real world it was a harsh sentence often given to women who murdered, or anyone who broke into a Christian Celt church.

5 d) Vicious criminals were sometimes drowned in swamps under a cover of wattle hurdles but this practice probably died out in the AD years. Drowning by trampling in a swamp also seems to have been a punishment for cowards and shirkers who left others to do all the work. So, next time your dad asks you to help with the washing up, make sure he's not a Celt before you refuse!

Did you know … ?

The Celts had a law against damaging trees. But your punishment depended on what sort of tree it was! You were in deep trouble if you harmed an oak, apple, ash, hazel, yew or fir tree. It was less serious if you damaged an alder, willow, birch or elm.

Weird words

The Celts couldn't write because their religious leaders wouldn't let them. Those Druids believed that the written word meant power. They kept calendars (with a month counted off each time the moon appeared) and marked off what days were good for things like invading Rome or sacrificing a cow.

Eventually the Celts made an alphabet similar to the Vikings. It was made up of straight lines because these letters were carved onto stone or wood. Historians have been able to learn something of Celt life from these carvings. The Welsh alphabet had 30 letters and looked like this:

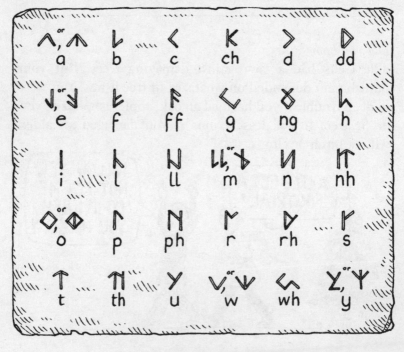

Being able to write is very useful. You can leave messages…

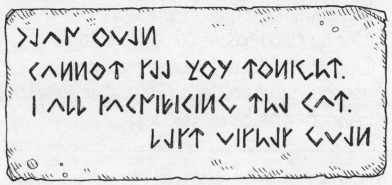

Rotten riddles

On the dark winter nights the Celts had no television to keep themselves amused. They were very fond of word games, though. In a room with just a fire it became a bit boring to do, 'I spy with my little eye something beginning with F.'

So the Celts had a good line in riddles – puzzles to which you had to guess the answer. Could *you* be a Celt Clever Clogs and solve this one … ?

In come two legs carrying one leg,
Lay down one leg on three legs,
Out go two legs, in come four legs,
Out go five legs, in come two legs,
Snatches up three legs, flings it at four legs
And brings back one leg.

The awful thing about riddles is that the answer is so easy once it's explained! The longer you think about it the more satisfying it is to get the answer in the end. So, DO NOT read the answer for 24 hours! Go and read something else ... the Bible, the *Encyclopaedia Britannica*, your sister's diary – anything.

Answer:
Well? Did you guess it? If not, did you spend 24 hours trying? No? You should be ashamed of yourself. Here's the answer ... A woman (two legs) comes in carrying a leg of lamb (one leg) and puts it down on a stool (three legs). In comes a dog (four legs) and runs off with it. Now, even you can work out the ending from there!

Celtic compass
The Celts were skilful sailors and needed a good sense of direction. After all, they didn't want to sail over the edge of the world which (as we can all see) is flat. But the Celtic

116

sailors didn't describe directions as North, South, East or West. They used colours. The sun rose in the 'purple' and by midday was in the 'white'. You too could become a geographical genius by learning this chart...

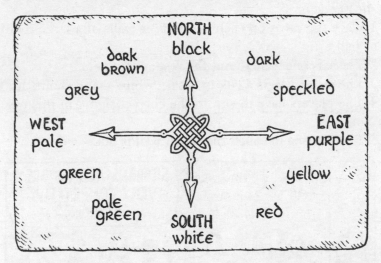

Celt compass games

Of course simply learning these directions is no fun. You have to use them. Try giving someone directions using the Celtic compass...

Game 1
You'll need:
- 10 or more players
- four signs saying North, South, East and West.

All you do is:

1 Place the cards on each of the four walls of a large room or hall.

2 There is one 'caller' and the rest are runners.

3 The caller selects a colour – say, 'white' – and shouts it.

4 The players have to run to the correct sign – in this case 'South'.

5 The last one to touch the south wall is out.

6 The game continues with one player dropping out each round. Obviously, the corners are the colours or shades between the main compass points. 'Dark' or 'Speckled' means north-east.

7 The winner is the last player in. Change callers and start again.

8 When the players are getting faster then add a new call ... 'Cut-throat!' This means 'freeze'. Everyone who moves after the call is out.

Game 2
You'll need:

- at least two players
- a room full of obstructions (like chairs)
- a scarf for a blindfold.

All you do is:

1 The aim is for the leader to get the blindfolded partner safely across the room to a target without bumping, breaking or even touching an obstruction in between. (It would also be nice if the blindfolded partner does not break a leg.)

2 The leader must talk the partner through the obstacles but can only use the Celt compass to do so.

3 'Black' becomes straight ahead, 'White' is backwards, 'Purple' is right and 'Pale' is left. 'Dark Brown' is a little to the left and 'Grey' is more to the left and so on.

4 The leader cannot use the word 'Stop' (or left, right, ahead or back) but they can add the word 'Cut-throat!' meaning 'Stop!'

5 Score 10 for a clear run to the target; deduct a point for every obstacle touched.

6 Change the blindfold to the leader and try again. The winner is the one with the highest score as leader.

7 If there is more than one pair, then the pairs can race from one end of the room to the other. Touching any obstacle means the pair must go back to the start.

8 The winner is the pair to reach the far-wall first. In the event of a tie the winner is the blindfolded partner with the fewest broken bones.

Sadly, the Celtic compass has died out. Otherwise we'd have had cowboys riding the range in the Wild Pale and polar bears at the Black Pole.

Manchester in the Grey of England (that sounds right) would be playing soccer against Pale Ham while you'd expect to see a lot of heather on the Purple coast of Scotland or buttercups in the Yellow part of Wales.

But what would we be eating two days after Good Friday? Purple-er eggs? Yeuch!

Did you know … ?
In travelling it is considered unlucky to travel anti-clockwise? The superstitious Celts always made sure they travelled in the same direction as the sun – clockwise or 'deosil' as they called it.

Want to get good marks in that test? Then walk round the

desk deosil before you sit down. Want that horrible history teacher to fall out of bed? Walk round his car 'widdershins' (that's anti-clockwise).

Remember that the number three is lucky for Celts and nine (that's three-threes) is magical. But walking round that desk nine times would probably make you too dizzy to see the exam paper!

Epilogue

Hopeless history
The Romans were horrible historians who tried to give the Celts a bad name. But for 1500 years every other historian has repeated the same 'fact'...

The Romans never reached Ireland

(Check your school history books and you're bound to find it there somewhere.)

How do the hopeless historians know the Romans never reached Ireland? Because the Romans never said they reached Ireland. This is not the same as the Romans saying they never reached Ireland.

DID YOU SAY YOU REACHED IRELAND OR DIDN'T YOU?!

I'M NOT SAYING

And now the truth can be told at last...

THE ROMANS REACHED IRELAND

The history books are all wrong ... except this one, of course, but we don't like to boast!

THE HERALD

CELTIC MYTH DESTROYED

MYTH DESTROYED HERE!

A dull piece of land near Dublin holds the key to a Celtic mystery that has lasted for nearly 2,000 years. A team of archaeologists have announced that they've been investigating a 40-acre patch of ground about 15 miles north of Dublin. The spot, called Drumanagh, is the site of a Roman coastal fort. Earth walls and ditches show where the fort was – coins, ornaments and jewellery show that Romans lived there. Coins of emperors Titus, Trajan and Hadrian show the Romans lived in Ireland from at least AD 79 till AD 138 and historians never knew … till now.

The fort has been described as the most important find in Irish history. But here's the really strange thing. The archaeologists knew the secret of the site in the 1980s and kept it hidden for over 10 years while they worked on it! Meanwhile thousands of children in hundreds of schools have been told, 'The Romans never reached Ireland.' Huh! Historians!

Could *you* keep the 'most important find in Irish history' a secret for over 10 years? The coins and valuables went to the National Museum of Ireland where they were hidden away. The archaeologists, historians and museum staff hid the truth from us. It makes you wonder what else historians know that they won't tell us? Is Adolf Hitler still alive? Did King Arthur really exist? Did King Henry I have his brother murdered? Did Humpty Dumpty fall off the wall … or was he pushed?

 STARTLING NEW EVIDENCE HAS COME TO LIGHT SUGGESTING THE BRICKS AT THE VERY TOP OF THE WALL MAY HAVE BEEN TAMPERED WITH

One day we may have answers to all of these questions…

The Celt comeback

The trouble with the Celts is they didn't bother to write much. So a lot of the things we hear about them were written by their enemies – people like the Romans. Would you trust *your* enemy to write good things about you?

Other things were written by people who did not approve of the Celts – people like the monks of the Middle Ages. The monks were Christian and the old Celts were not. You're not going to get a good school report from a teacher who doesn't approve of you!

Still the Roman writers seemed to respect these wild, strange people. Lucretius wrote...

> *And this race of people from the plains were as hard as the hard land they came from; they were built on firmer, stronger bones and given mighty muscles. They were a race unafraid of the heat or the cold, of the plague or of strange foods. For many years they led their lives among the beasts of the earth and were not tamed.*

But the people who were 'tamed' – the Romans – were able to defeat these heroic people. A Greek writer, Strabo, claimed that their fearless nature made them easy to outwit...

> *The Celt race is madly fond of war and quick to do battle. Otherwise they are honest and not evil characters. And so when they are stirred up they assemble in their bands for battle, quite openly and without careful planning. As a result they are easily handled by those who want to outwit them. For the Celts are always ready to face danger, even if they have nothing on their side but their own strength and courage.*

Strength and courage and honesty were not enough and as the years went by the Celts were driven back from the richest countries by enemies with more cunning and greed.

Of course, Strabo also pointed out that the Celts had some horrible historical habits...

> *There are also other accounts of their human sacrifices; for they used to shoot men down with arrows, or making a large statue of straw and wood, throw into it cattle and all sorts of wild animals and human beings and thus make a burnt offering.*

But at least the Celts left behind many good things they made and we know they were great artists. They also left behind their ancestors who still live in Ireland, Scotland, Brittany (France) and Cornwall (England). And though the spiky, dyed hair is gone some of the mystic powers seem to remain in some of them.

It's sad that the cunning and greedy have taken the world from the honest and courageous. Maybe one day a leader will appear who will lead the world back to the ways of courage and honesty. Maybe his name will be … Arthur! It would be nice to think so. It's something to hope for, anyway.

CUT-THROAT CELTS

CELTS

GRISLY QUIZ

**Now find out if you're a
Cut-throat Celts expert!**

It's a Curious Celtic Life...

So – reckon you know all about this terrible tribe, with all their curious customs and peculiar practices? Take this quick quiz and find out.

1. England was created when the Angles and the Saxons took over the south-east of Britain in AD 520. What did they call their new land?
a) Angle-land
b) Saxonia
c) Engal-land

2. What was the name of the largest Celt tribe that fought the Romans?
a) Celtics
b) Gauls
c) Zulus

3. Why did the Celts cut off people's heads in battle?
a) They believed that they gained their enemy's wisdom and strength
b) They wanted to look down their enemy's throats
c) They wanted to eat them

4. Kissing under the mistletoe is a Celtic tradition, but the Celts only believed the mistletoe was magical when...
a) It was cut on the first day of July under a full moon
b) It was cut by a Druid using a gold sickle
c) It was plucked from a bough by a magpie

5. The Celts believed that the Druids had magical powers, but which of the following was not a Druid power?

a) Changing the weather
b) Time–travelling
c) Flying

6. The Celts believed in sacrificing people to keep their gods happy. How was the practice of 'death by air' carried out?
a) The victim was suffocated
b) The victim was strangled
c) The victim was hung

7. The first Celts lived during the Iron Age. Did this mean that...
a) They were good at getting the creases out of their favourite tunics
b) They used iron for making tools and weapons
c) They used iron bars for money

8. If you were round at a Celt's house and you smelt cedar oil coming from a chest, what would you find inside?
a) Nice-smelling blankets
b) Christmas presents
c) Heads

Bonkers Beliefs

The Celts were a crazy bunch. If you met one on the street and they told you the following facts, would you believe them? See if you can tell the troublesome truth from the foolish fiction.

1. 'I've just thrown my favourite sheep off the cliff so the gods will bless me with more sheep.'

2. 'Can't stop. I'm off to get my nails done.'

3. 'My best friend just died, so I'm off round his place for a good cry.'

4. 'Would you mind holding my clothes while I nip off and fight a battle?'

5. 'Hang on ... Just remembered. I'm not fighting today – I spotted a crane earlier.'

6. 'We've spent all year growing corn, and now that we've harvested it we're going to bury it.'

7. 'I'm off to help St Brannoc build a church because he found a cow and her calf there – and that's magic he says.'

8. 'I've just turned sixteen so I've been turfed out of me mum and dad's and made to live with another family.

COULD YOU BE A CELT?

Now you've found out all about Celts, how do you think you'd fare in the evil Iron Age? Take this quiz and find out if the Celts would welcome you as a warrior or sacrifice you by suffocation...

1. The Celts bathed every day, but would you be able to play with your rubber duck in peace? (Clue: It's a family affair)

2. You know all about Halloween, of course, but what would you do on 31 October if you were a Celt? (Clue: It's not a trick question)

3. If you were a Celtic sailor, what do you think would keep you from drowning? (Clue: A bird in the hand…)

4. If you were involved in a game of hurling with some ancient warriors, what would you use as a ball? (Clue: Use your head!)

5. You'd have to learn to fight fiercely, but who'd be teaching you? (Clue: Dress-ed to kill)

6. The Celts were good at finding their way around. They used a compass with colours to show direction. If you were off in a purple direction, which way would you be heading? (Clue: Into the sunrise)

7. Playing apple-bobbing on Halloween, you see a girl stick the apple pips on her face. What on Earth is she doing? (Clue: It's a horrible husband Halloween habit)

8. If a Celtic woman asked you to pick her up some make-up, where would you go? (Clue: It's a *berry* simple question...)

Answers

It's a Curious Celtic Life...

1a) They called it Angle-land, which eventually became England.

2b) Roman Ammianus Marcellinus noted that the Gauls were fierce, argued a lot and were proud.

3a) They believed that a person's power was all in their head – even if they were dead!

4b) They believed that the oak tree was holy and the mistletoe that grew on it had magical powers

5c) Druids could also (they said) change their shape to anything they wanted and bring down mists to make themselves invisible ... but they couldn't fly.

6a,b or c) Sacrificing to the God of air was carried out by suffocation, as well as hanging and strangulation.

7b) Iron was the magnificent metal of this era and was used for all sorts of things – tools, pots, jewellery – you name it.

8c) The Celts liked to keep heads as trophies, and would preserve them in cedar oil.

Bonkers Beliefs

1. True – the Celts believed that by sacrificing animals the gods would look favourably on them.

2. True – wealthy Celts were big on manicures!

3. False – when somebody died the Celts threw a big party and had a right old laugh!
4. True – the Celts often fought naked, probably to scare their opponents. Not the wisest thing to do in the winter…
5. True – seeing a crane (the bird not the lifting machine) was unlucky, they thought, and Celtic warriors used it as an excuse to pack up and go home!
6. Totally true – it seems like a daft idea, but placing the grain in the ground it kept it fresh until it was needed.

7. Almost true – St B built a church on the site where he found a sow and her piglets, not a cow. He was told to build it in a dream.
8. False – he would have been moved out at the age of seven! This was meant to teach Celtic kids that they were part of a tribe, not just a family.

Could you be a Celt?
1. Not a chance. Better hope you were part of a small family as you'd all have to share your time in the tub.
2. You'd dress in a scary costume to ward off the spirits. No trick or treating, though.
3. A feather from a wren – especially if the feather had come from a bird that had been killed on New Year's Day.
4. Chances are you'd be throwing round the head of one of your enemies. Don't try this at school…

5. A woman – the men were too busy so the women taught fighting.

6. You'd be heading east (as long as you weren't colour blind).

7. She'd be trying to find out the name of her future husband. She'd name each of the pips and the last to fall off would be the name of the person she was going to marry.

8. No – not the local supermarket! You'd go to the woods. The juice from herbs and berries was used as make-up.

INTERESTING INDEX

Where will you find 'bad breath',
'inspecting entrails' and 'underpants' in an index?
In a Horrible Histories book, of course!

138

139

Terry Deary was born at a very early age, so long ago he can't remember. But his mother, who was there at the time, says he was born in Sunderland, north-east England, in 1946 – so it's not true that he writes all *Horrible Histories* from memory. At school he was a horrible child only interested in playing football and giving teachers a hard time. His history lessons were so boring and so badly taught, that he learned to loathe the subject. *Horrible Histories* is his revenge.

Martin Brown was born in Melbourne, on the proper side of the world. Ever since he can remember he's been drawing. His dad used to bring back huge sheets of paper from work and Martin would fill them with doodles and little figures. Then, quite suddenly, with food and water, he grew up, moved to the UK and found work doing what he's always wanted to do: drawing doodles and little figures.